LIFE WITHOUT THE BANK

FOR THOSE QUESTIONING THE TRADITIONAL FINANCIAL SYSTEM AND WHY YOU SHOULD!

MARY JO IRMEN
BEST SELLING AUTHOR OF FARMING WITHOUT THE BANK

Copyright 2020 by Mary Jo Irmen All rights reserved

No part of this publication may be reproduced, stored in a retrieval system, or transmitted in any way or by any means, electronic, mechanical, photocopy, recording, or otherwise, without the prior permission of the publisher, except as provided by U.S. copyright law. Please send inquires to maryjo@withoutthebank.com

---

ISBN: 978-0-9907052-7-7

FiscalBridge, LLC- Life Without the Bank
P.O. Box 2351, Bismarck, ND 50502-2351
Email: maryjo@withhoutthebank.com
Website: www.withoutthebank.com
Phone: 701-751-3917

Cover design by Cyberdogz Marketing
Cover image used provided by iStock

Printed in the United States of America

This book is dedicated to all those small business owners and workers who make the world go round.

To you, I also wish much wealth and health.

Mary Jo

CONTENTS

Acknowledgments

CHAPTER 1 - The American Financial Dream   1

CHAPTER 2 - Conditioned Thinking   4

   Change Your Thought Process 4

CHAPTER 3 - Honesty, Handling and Storage of Money 7

   Money - Respect 7

   Compartmentalizing Money 8

   Storing Money For Growth 10

CHAPTER 4 - Payments And Interest 11

   Volume Of Interest vs. Rate Of Interest 11

CHAPTER 5 - Cash is Not King 13

   Uninterrupted Compound Interest 14

CHAPTER 6 - Banks Control 18

   Control 18

   Accessibility 19

   Killing The Savers 20

   Spread Of Money 21

CHAPTER 7 - Wall Street Scam 24

   Investments 24

   Rates Of Return 26

   Hang In There, It'll Recover 27

Management Fees 29

The Math 33

Free Money 34

Taxes And Retirement 37

Retirement Distribution 40

Market History Performance 42

Contract With The Government 43

CHAPTER 8 - A Better way To Pay For College 44

CHAPTER 9 - It's All How You Think 47

Whole Life Versus Other Permanent Products 49

Term Insurance 53

CHAPTER 10 - Cash Surrender Value 57

Access To Cash Value 57

Borrowing Against Cash Value 58

Dividends 59

CHAPTER 11 - Protection 60

More Than Collateral 60

Key-Man Policy 61

CHAPTER 12 - Policy Understanding 63

Guaranteed and Non-Guaranteed Assumptions 63

Contract Premium 63

Net Cash Value 64

Death Benefit 64

Cum(ulative) Premium 65

Annual Dividend 65

Increase In Net Cash Value 65

CHAPTER 13 - Young Versus Old 66

Cash Value 66

Death Benefit 67

Policies On Young Children 68

CHAPTER 14 - Case Studies 70

Case Study - Using Your Life Insurance Today 71

Case Study - Supplementing Retirement 75

Case Study - Teens And Young Adults 78

Case Study - Grandchild's Policy 83

Case Study - Using Inheritance Or Large Sums Of Cash 84

Family Banking 86

CHAPTER 15 - Your Next Step 88

Do Your Due Diligence 89

Frequently Asked Questions 90

Notes 93

About The Author 94

Recommended Readings 95

Diclaimer 95

Notes (Writing Space) 96

Acknowledgments

"Tell me and I forget. Teach me and I remember. Involve me and I learn."
- Benjamin Franklin

A simple thank you to all my farm clients who pushed me into writing another book. Lord knows I did not set out to be a writer. But, as an advocate for the people who want to know more, I have written this book to share with you information that isn't readily found, much less presented in laymen's terms.

Second and most importantly, thank you to R. Nelson Nash for sharing this concept with all of us. Without his book, *Becoming Your Own Banker*, my life would have never changed and you would not be reading this.

Finally, thanks to my amazing husband for supporting and believing in me. I am a firm believer that without your patience and support, I would not be where I am today.

CHAPTER ONE

The American Financial Dream

"Either I will find a way or I will create a way; but I will not create an excuse."
- Unknown

You all hear about it - living the American Dream. This can mean different things to different people, but I want to talk to you about the financial dreams of many Americans. This dream for so many means having no financial stress today, owning a business, enough for retirement, and avoiding having to use the banks.

The American Dream was sold to me in high school as - go to college, get a good job, stick money into your 401k and retire happily ever after. So I did go to college (because the company I worked for paid for it) and received my business degree. There I was, living the American Dream with a decent job that had great benefits and a retirement plan option.

Yet, I was not buying into this. I knew from everything I was reading that the stock market was not going to make me wealthy. Nor did it make sense to me. No one, not even my employers, could explain to me what stocks to invest in to make money. When I asked them they had no clue, they just trusted the advisors. Well, if it was good enough for them it should be ok, right? After all they were CPAs, they should know. Then it happened in 2008. The market crashed. I called my advisor and she said leave it there, it'll come back. I left it and by the end of 2010 I had 50 percent of what I started with!

Nope, this was NOT my thing, nor was it working. All I could think is who in their right mind would put their hard-earned money into this system just to lose it?

At the end of 2010 I came across a book called, *Becoming Your Own Banker*, by R. Nelson Nash. He was teaching the Infinite Banking Concept®, a way to think about money correctly, create your own bank, be the banker, and create wealth outside of Wall Street. I could hardly believe it.

If this was true, why hadn't anyone told me about this?

Well, it turned out to be true and it just made sense. There are two groups that understand money. Who are those people handling the money and building a new building on every corner? Banks. That is where the majority of our money is stored. Think about it, all your income runs through the bank. When you need something you either take from your savings account or go to banks to borrow "their" money. Banks are the wealthiest business in town. They are in the business of lending your money to others, or better yet lending your money back to you! (I will explain more as we go through this book.)

If this is where all the money is stored, why aren't we thinking like a banker or trying to be the banker? I had never heard of that, not even with all the books on investing I had read. Imagine what life would be like if you owned the bank. Imagine what it would be like if you were the banker, the one making decisions about lending money to yourself and setting the terms of that loan. What a glorious life! You would be in control.

The other group that understands money is the wealthy. Many often get angry with these people, but I challenge you to stop and ask questions of them. I always say, "jealousy kills curiosity," many are so busy being jealous they don't stop to question how these people created wealth. What I have found is that wealthy people do not stick their money into the stock market. They put their money where it's accessible and into things they understand and control.

They might buy businesses, real estate, or even farmland, etc. Warren Buffett is quoted as saying "never invest in something you don't understand."

As R. Nelson Nash said in his book, "If we take all the money in the world and divide it equally, within a short few years the poor will be poor and the wealthy will be wealthy." Why? Because they understand how money works. They think differently.

If you want to be wealthy you must think like the wealthy. You must own the bank, be the banker, and must have access to liquid money. If you are reading this book it's because you are in search of answers. Congrats to you!

You will find the answers in this book. The biggest challenge for most of us is that no one puts it into terms where the you's and me's can understand it. This book will be different. There will be no fancy financial terms. I prefer to keep things simple, so people know what I am talking about. For you to better understand, we are first going to go over your thought process and then get into numbers. They are both equally as important, but the way you think is far more important. Keep this in mind as you move forward.

CHAPTER TWO

Conditional Thinking

"You don't fix your problems. You fix your thinking. Then problems fix themselves."
- Steve Mehr

As you continue reading, keep this thought in mind, "You can lead humans to knowledge, but you can't make them think." What you are going to learn is nothing you've ever been told before and it is going to lead you to question things, as it did me. Moving forward, **you must use imagination, reason and logic to envision how this concept can be used.** Keep in mind you need to think like a banker, be the banker, and be the one holding the wealth. If you don't think from this state, you may miss the entire concept.

By the end of the book you will be asking yourself why you haven't heard about this before, and depending on your age, you may ask, "Where were you 20 years ago?"

CHANGE YOUR THOUGHT PROCESS

Have you ever heard someone say, "There is no other way," this is what I call conditioned thinking. It's accepting everything you hear as truth. This is how most of us are with our money. We just believe what others tell us. You hear things like:

- Live within your means.
- Save up and pay cash.

- Borrow money from the bank because money is cheap.
- Chase rates of return in the stock market for the best way to create retirement.

Conditioned thinking doesn't allow us to question if these things are right or wrong. Do you ever ask:
- How can I have more?
- Is there a better way to use my cash?
- Is there a better way to save for retirement?

Albert Einstein said, "The important thing is not to stop questioning. Curiosity has its own reason for existing." Never questioning a thought process does not leave a lot of room for logic or advancement.

You have been magnificently conditioned to think you need the banks for purchases and the stock market for retirement. Just like trainers condition elephants to believe they are inescapably tethered by a small rope, society has us believing we are tethered to the banks and stock market.

Financial gurus would like us to think money is hard to understand. It's not. It's simple, and as my client Nate said, **"This is really easy when you stop making it so hard."**

You never want to get to a position where you think you know it all. This is called the Arrival Syndrome, where your mind becomes closed to anything new. No one wants to be that guy, the know-it-all who really doesn't know it all. Daniel Boorstin said it well, "The greatest obstacle to discovering the shape of the earth, the continents, and the oceans was not ignorance - it was the illusion of knowledge."

I hope you are open to a challenge and learning.

The only way to advance yourself financially is to beat both of these. As you share this book and concept with others, you will quickly notice those with conditioned thinking and the arrival syndrome. They will be the ones with comments like, "It is too good to be true," "I have enough money and don't need this," or "that's a terrible place to put money."

Thomas Edison said, "Five percent of the people think; 10 percent of the people think they think; and the other 85 percent would rather die than think." When you look at those 85 percent, are they conditioned to not ask questions, or have they truly arrived and believe their thinking days are over? There is a big difference between not questioning and knowing it all. Oftentimes, those who don't question have given in to conditioned thinking but are still very teachable.

CHAPTER THREE

Honesty, Handling and Storage of Money

"No man should receive a dollar unless that dollar has been fairly earned."
- Theodore Roosevelt

Two factors never addressed in finances are being honest with our money and the best place to store money.

MONEY - RESPECT

When you borrow money from the bank, credit card company, or even a friend, you pay them back plus interest - high interest in some cases. You'd never think to skip out on a payment, they'd either come take back what is theirs or report you to the credit bureau.

Yet, when you take money from your savings account to make a purchase you don't even consider paying it back PLUS interest. **You are stealing from yourself and you don't even realize it. Why is the bank or credit card company more important than you?** Because you have NEVER even considered it. No one has ever mentioned it.

If you are using cash, chances are you are a saver and you will continue to save by continuing to make deposits into your savings account. Keep making those deposits PLUS interest. Imagine yourself as the bank and the banker. If you lent that same money to someone else, would you charge interest? Most likely you would, and if you don't you are a terrible banker. No one charges zero percent, not even those credit card companies and car dealerships.

Today, as I write this, your savings account doesn't pay worth a darn. You may get .25 percent interest. Yet, when you took it out to buy furniture you LOST that .25 percent. If nothing else, why not pay yourself back PLUS the .25 percent you would have earned had you left it in there. Anything above that is more savings!

To further my point, let's look at an example. You want new furniture and want to pay cash for it, so you save $5,000. In order to have this money in savings, you put it there through monthly savings contributions. Once the $5,000 is there, you withdraw the money to buy your furniture and your account is now at zero. You decide not to continue saving because you met your end result. If you are thinking like a banker and being honest with your money, you will be diligent and make payments into your savings account to replace the $5,000 you took and pay interest back on that money.

When you pay yourself back the $5,000 plus interest, your account grows by the interest amount. You once again have the $5,000 plus interest to use again for another purchase. You've now created wealth by being an honest banker.

You may be saying, "I don't want payments." However, if that payment is putting money back so you can use it again, isn't it really a deposit? Don't let the terminology confuse you.

This is a great start to the **concept** of life without the bank where you become the banker and the owner of the bank.

COMPARTMENTALIZING MONEY

Now that you are thinking like an honest banker and understand that your money has value, we can move into the storage of money.

Do you have separate savings accounts designated just for vacation and let's say that new furniture? If so, I want to know why that or any account is set up for just a single intention?

I call this compartmentalizing money. This has been taught to us by the so-called financial gurus. Have an envelope for the Christmas fund, college fund, vacation, etc. If one comes up short, no borrowing from the other. Now, I can understand this logic when you are separating business from personal expenses, but it's rare this needs to be done outside of that.

You do not need to compartmentalize money if you are an honest banker and pay it back, like we discussed earlier. It can all be stored in one account. There is only one pool of money in the world; in your household and in your business. Money is meant to flow and will do just that when you borrow and pay back. That way it's there to use again later for another purchase.

I love it when my clients say they can't pay a loan off because then they won't have money for an emergency. Yet they have access to other money, just not in the designated savings account. It's all one pool!

Now, let's tie it all together to see how it works. You have a general savings account and have been saving for next year's vacation. You currently have $5,000 in there. Before the vacation comes you need $1,000 worth of new tires on your vehicle, so you borrow money from your vacation fund account to buy the tires. Over the next year you are honest and you put $1,000 back plus 10 percent interest into the savings account. You now have $5,100 to go on vacation. See how that vacation fund was not just for vacation, and it grew by $100? That money was used for both vacation and tires because you were an honest banker. No need to compartmentalize.

This honesty mindset will also allow you to manage debt better. If you don't have the obligation to repay yourself, you tend to overspend. If you are honest and repay yourself, you realize you can't buy it if you can't afford the payment back to yourself, just as you wouldn't buy something you can't afford to repay to a bank.

STORING MONEY FOR GROWTH

Where you store this money is very important. Most of us only know of the obvious places, like savings, CDs or investment accounts. If you don't use the right storage account you can't use it like I described above.

You want to make sure you can put your money where it is safe, earns uninterrupted compound interest and remains liquid so you can use it at any time without question or penalty. In the next few chapters I will break this all down further.

CHAPTER FOUR

Payments and Interest

> *"Rule No. 1: Never lose money.*
> *Rule No. 2: Never forget Rule No. 1."*
> - Warren Buffett

VOLUME OF INTEREST VS. RATE OF INTEREST

Typical conditioned thinking is that if you can't pay cash for it, just borrow the money, and as long as the payment is affordable, it's all good.

If you are like most of my clients, you don't even know the interest rate on your small loans, such as cars, boats, campers, etc. Our thought process is the **interest rate** is small and the loan, if only for a few years, is no big deal. Yet, when you purchase a home, your rate may even be less than that car, boat or camper loan. But you want to get that paid off as quickly as possible because the **volume of interest** over 30 years will double your home cost.

Now what if you looked at ALL your small loans that same way and added up the interest you paid over five years on the car, over the six years on the boat and over 10 years of that camper. You are not done there. Add those all up and **think about the amount of lost interest over your lifetime!** The volume of interest you pay far outweighs the rate of interest you are taught to pay attention to. This is how banks make money and why they have so much of it.

You don't stop buying things until you are dead (and even then they say you're not done because of the funeral). But, you can stop giving interest money to others and instead pay it back to an entity you own and control.

With the amount you spend on mortgages, student loans, car loan, credit card payments, business loans, and vacations, anything saved is a further advancement to your financial system. It is necessary when building your bank.

If you are in your 50s, I challenge you to add up the volume of interest you have lost over the years. If you are younger than that, I encourage you to estimate what you will lose over your lifetime if you keep doing what you are doing. What would this money have done or do for you? It may have given you the ability to start your own business, buy investment property, travel more or retire sooner.

Interestingly, business owners know the amount of interest they pay each year because they get to write it off for taxes. That interest payment may be the difference between making a profit or not.

I can't say it enough - It's not the percentage of interest, it's the volume of interest. Start thinking of your payments as two parts and keep track of the volume of interest that is leaving your hands.

Get more information by listening to Mary Jo's podcast, Without the Bank.

CHAPTER FIVE

Cash is Not King

"There is only one class in the community that thinks more about money than the rich, and that is the poor."
- Oscar Wilde

We have talked about using cash to buy things and pay yourself back so now I'm going to be burst your bubble and tell you cash is not king. Don't close the book!

Warning - this is the hardest thing to grasp if you are a cash buyer - but hang in there. You have likely been conditioned to think of cash as king. Save until you have the cash you need to make your purchases. This idea is not wrong. It is better than losing interest through financing, as we just talked about. But it is not king. Instead, I like to say cash is queen.

My mentor R. Nelson Nash says it perfectly in his book, Becoming Your Own Banker, "**You finance everything that you buy - you either pay interest to someone else or you give up interest you could have earned otherwise.**" Take a minute to reread that and think about it.

This in finance technical terms is called **lost opportunity cost** - something very real and important that you have never been taught.

For example, if you are purchasing a boat with cash, it means you took that cash from an interest-bearing account and gave up the ability to have that money earn anything in exchange for a depreciating asset. In essence, **you've lost the opportunity to make money on that money - lost opportunity cost.** Cash has a cost.

UNINTERRUPTED COMPOUND INTEREST

Chart 5-1 on page 14 below illustrates the power of having your money earn **uninterrupted** compound interest versus the cost of using cash.

CHART 5-1

Annual Contribution	$15,000.00
Rate of Return	4%
Time (Years)	30
Number of Purchases	6
Years to Save for Purchase	4
Results	
Future Value	$841,274.08
Lost Interest	($760,029.24)

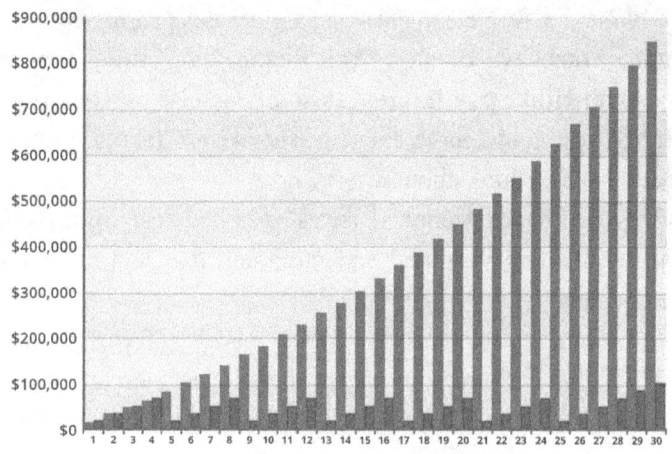

Let's say you were to save $15,000 each year in two different accounts. One account is where your money never left and the other is a savings account. After four years, withdraw that money out of savings to buy a new vehicle then repeat the cycle for 30 years. You can see each time you take money from savings you stop earning interest and interrupt the growth. You are always having to start over.

Look at the other column, where your money is earning uninterrupted compound interest and just keeps growing. You would have had an extra $760,029.24 had you not interrupted that growth. This is what the wealthy know that you do not know. You must use a tool that allows your money to do this and it is not a savings account. Cash has a cost.

Another example of the true cost of cash is to look at Chart 5-2. Should you use $100,000 cash as a down payment on a home? Had that money been able to grow at 4 percent over a lifetime you would have had a total of $710,668. If you used this cash, you would have lost the opportunity to have the extra $610,668. This is the true cost of the house down payment.

CHART 5-2

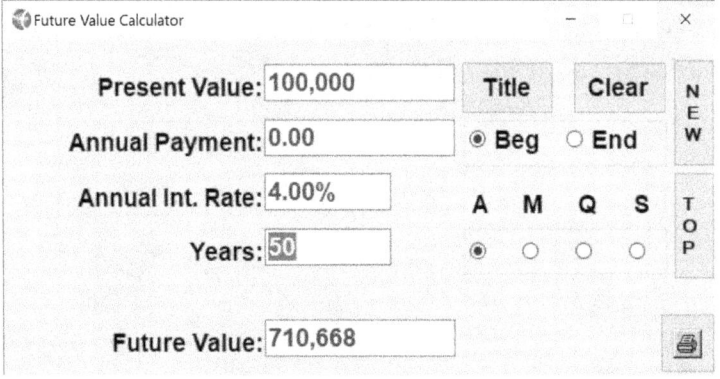

Again, this is what R. Nelson Nash is referring to when he says you finance everything you buy, even when you pay cash.

As you can see, interruption of growth is a huge factor when it comes to creating wealth. Yet, it is not even talked about. All you hear about is compound interest, in fact Albert Einstein said, "Compound interest is the eighth wonder of the world. He who understands it, earns it... he who doesn't, pays it." I wish Einstein would have added the word "uninterrupted" before "compound interest" - that is the game changer.

You may have seen this but I love the illustration shown on Chart 5-3 on page 17 of doubling a penny every day to show the effects of compounding money. Looking at the chart, it only takes 28 days to get to a million dollars, but look what happens if you keep going. By day 31, there is $10 million dollars! As you see, 80 percent of your compounding happens in the last three days. That is the power of long-term uninterrupted compounding.

Think about it. The two places where this interruption happens most are savings accounts and market falls - the places where you are told to put money first!

There is no denying the power of uninterrupted compounding. You would not want to have the growth of your business interrupted, go backwards, and then have to work back up to where you were. The same is true with your personal finances. Yet, that is what you are doing with your money.

CHART 5-3

Uninterrupted Compounding of a Penny			
Day	Amount	Day	Amount
1	$0.01	17	$655.36
2	$0.02	18	$1,310.72
3	$0.04	19	$2,621.44
4	$0.08	20	$5,242.88
5	$0.16	21	$10,485.76
6	$0.32	22	$20,971.52
7	$0.64	23	$41,943.04
8	$1.28	24	$83,886.08
9	$2.56	25	$167,772.16
10	$5.12	26	$335,544.32
11	$10.24	27	$671,088.64
12	$20.48	28	$1,342,177.28
13	$40.96	29	$2,684,354.56
14	$81.92	30	$5,368,709.12
15	$163.84	31	$10,737,418.24
16	$327.68		

CHAPTER SIX

Banks Control

"If you think nobody cares if you're alive, try missing a couple car payments."
- Earl Wilson

Banks are in business, just like any other business, to make money. The only difference with their business is they make money off of your money!

Many people get frustrated because banks want so much control. But think about it - if you were lending money to someone wouldn't you want something for collateral and wouldn't you check to be sure the borrower could pay? Banks do not want property of any kind, they want incoming cash flow in the form of payments or deposits.

Cash flow is imperative to the bank's financial health. Each time banks receive a dollar they are able to borrow 10 times that from the Federal Reserve. They then have $9 to lend to you and charge you interest on it! The bank made interest on $9 that never existed! This is called fractional reserve banking, and if you are not familiar with it I suggest you check it out on YouTube. This should explain why banks are all fighting for your business. The more deposits and payments they get, the better for them.

CONTROL

We all love banks for deposits and checking, but loans can be a different story. They can be very controlling and nearly impossible to work with when you need them the most.

Payback terms are controlled by them, the lenders, not you, the borrower. When you borrow money from banks, you have essentially agreed to a business partnership where you no longer independently control what you bought. Instead, you put it up as collateral to the loan. Should you default on the loan, they are going to take that collateral. The bank is your partner who has majority power, as they should, because they put up the funds. As the saying goes, those with the gold make the rules.

When you are making payments to banks you are essentially working for THEM. When the bank makes money off the interest, the bank shareholders and owners get the profit! It should be your goal to become part owner of the bank so you can share in the profits. If you're not already thinking, "How do I do that?" you should be.

ACCESSIBILITY

Think about how easy it would be to get money if you owned the bank. Liquid accessible money is what is important in time of need, and that is the worst time to be at someone else's mercy. Over the years, I have heard many stories of people needing money when times were bad, yet they had nowhere to go, not even borrowing against the equity of their homes.

Just because you have equity in your home does not mean you can access that money. Many banks will deny you access to it if you started a business and don't have two to three years of financials to prove you have the income to make the payment. If you are retired and want to refinance your home, you can't do that because you can't prove you can make the loan repayment. It's the same if you lost your job and need access to that money - no income to make payments means no loan. And finally, banks have been known to pull back on lending when the economy isn't doing well. These scenarios are all too risky for the bank. Remember, they want cash flow, not a hard asset they will have to sell.

The money is there, but it's not liquid and is subject to bank approval. What good does this equity do you when you need to physically sell the home and move to get access to it? You know that will not happen at the perfect timing either. Equity in a home is not liquid money.

As a financially set individual, you may feel this doesn't apply to you because you have great history and you have never defaulted on a loan. To some extent you do have a little advantage, because you have established credit and years of history behind you. Regardless of your credit and history, you still have to prove you can make payments. Even if you can, you may be denied the loan.

A good example of this is a friend of mine who had amazing credit, payment history and money in the bank, yet in 2008 when the housing market crashed, they removed his line of credit on his house! He had not been using that line of credit and when he went to use it, he found out it was not accessible. The bank pulled his and everyone else's lines of credit. Even today, as I write this in 2020, the big banks are once again pulling lines of credit.

Don't be fooled. Good credit and payment history aren't guarantees when the one with the money is in control and can change the rules. You want to store money where it remains liquid.

KILLING THE SAVERS

Low interest rates are killing those who save and encouraging spending, which in turn increases household debt. Savers are looking for places to put money that pays decent rates. Those places used to be certificate of deposits. Depending on your age, you may or may not remember certificates of deposit (CDs). Many of today's young people have no idea what they are because the banks no longer pay you anything to deposit money into them. This was a great place to put money, and people even used them as collateral to loans because CDs make compound interest.

Savings accounts used to pay you something, too. Now many people don't bother. Low interest rates are a win for the bank and a win for those borrowing money to purchase things, but they are not a win for the saver. I have a few clients who have coffee cans filled with money, because they aren't making anything in the bank, and they are not too sure they can trust the bank. To each his own, but, if they planted it, they may have a better chance of it growing than waiting for the Federal Reserve to increase rates.

SPREAD OF MONEY

The banks are not wanting to raise rates because they make more money when rates are lower. The spread is yet another misconception no one bothers to clear up, until now.

In the 1980s, savers were earning 14 percent in their savings accounts, and the banks were lending money at 23 percent. Look at Chart 6-1 on page 22. Most people would say, "The bank made 9 percent," when in fact it made 64.29 percent as you can see on the next page. It's just a nine-point spread.

So what are they making today? Look at Chart 6-2 on page 22. Let's give banks the benefit of the doubt today and say they are giving us .75 percent on our savings. They then lend it to us at 3.5 percent. When you look at that you think "Wow, they are only making 2.75 percent." But, in fact, they are making 366.67 percent as you see below. They are making more with a smaller spread!

What if the spread was the same 9 points and they charged you 8.25 percent interest on your loan? They would be making 1,000 percent!

CHART 6-1

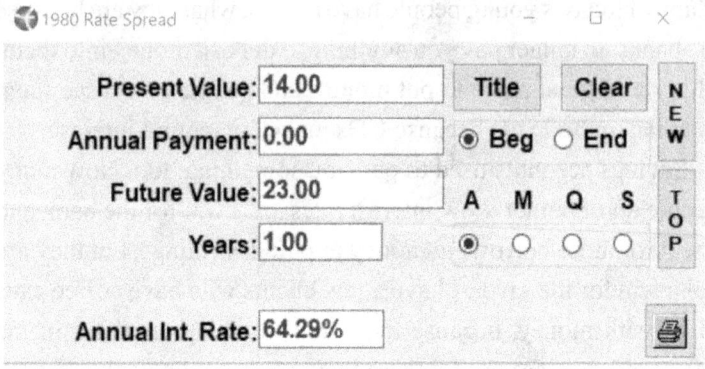

CHART 6-2

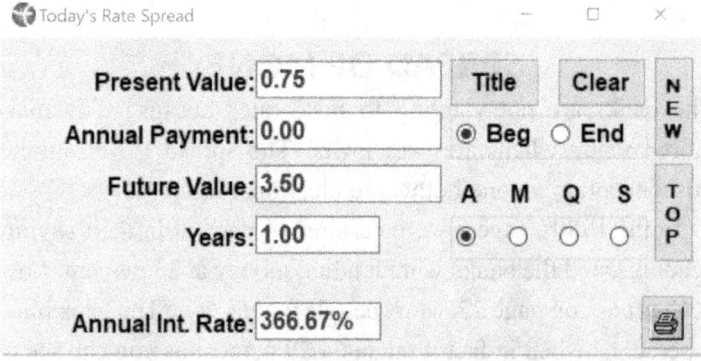

Think about it this way - If I bought a hammer for $0.75 and sold it to you for $3.50, I did not mark that hammer up $2.75. I marked that hammer up 366.67 percent. The same thing applies to spreads at the bank. They would like you to think it's a 2.75 percent spread but it's much better than that.

Many believe the banks will raise interest rates and are fearful things will always go up. Yet, after you see this, why would they? They make far more money when rates are lower. Plus, the media tells us it helps our economy to have low rates, people buy more.

Of course they buy more - the common theme is, "I can hardly afford not to buy it." I have even heard people say, "it's almost like they are giving it to me."

This is just the thinking they want you to have. Get those hard-working Americans into the stores so they can rack up debt. Low rates help banks, keep money flowing, and do nothing but create more consumer debt. We have more consumer debt now than we have ever had in history. It was $14.3 trillion in May 2020. Then when the Covid crisis hit and people were without work, two weeks without pay was a crisis. In my opinion, this happens because people over buy. It is easy because payments are affordable - as long as money is coming in. **Cash flow is king**, without it low rates and easy payments mean nothing.

In 2018, I read and heard banks were back in trouble for over-lending. Many do not have the collateral they need in relation to the loans they have on the books. I am seeing this firsthand with clients whose banks are calling notes or not releasing collateral when the loan is paid off.

No one is winning outside of the bank. Savers are being hurt because there isn't a good spot to put money and the general public is getting hurt from pure deception.

Get more information by listening to Mary Jo's podcast, Without the Bank.

CHAPTER SEVEN

Wall Street Scam

"You can be young without money, but you can't be old without it."
- Tennessee Williams

INVESTMENTS

Let's be clear from the onset of this chapter that I am NOT a financial advisor. One does not have to be more than capable of doing math and research to figure out what is going on with our investments. Think about this - you are conditioned to believe that you need to put your money into a stock market investment, chasing rates of return, while at the same time going to a lender to borrow money in order to buy things you need today. Likewise, you are conditioned to believe if you want to save for retirement you must chase rates of return, give up liquidity of money until age 59½ and accept risk.

As an employee and business owner, the only option given for retirement is to contribute to that stock-market-driven 401k, 403B, IRA or Roth IRA. If you are the business owner, you are not shown other options for employees!

Many ask why they have not heard of the Infinite Banking Concept® before. That answer may be found in a book by Rick Beuter, The Great Wall Street Retirement Scam. It is the best little book I have read to explain the history of Wall Street. He tells us IRAs and 401ks **began** in the mid-1970s and early 1980s.

At this time there was a change in how retirement for employees was managed. Employers used to manage the retirement account and use annuities to do so. This method gave the employees a guaranteed plan and the insurance company carried the risk. The change moved the risk from the employer to the employee and left the employee with no guarantees. During this change, employers were also given incentives to offer these new retirement accounts. One must question anything for which the government offers incentives.

Before all this change, hard-working Americans saved in traditional savings accounts, purchased certificates of deposit (CDs), or bought whole life insurance, to name a few. Wealthy were the only people investing in the stock market.

During this process of moving retirement accounts into the market, the stock market soared and huge rates of returns (ROR) were seen. These large rates of return drove the theory that the market was the place to be in order to make money, and that was true **at that time**. Years later you are seeing the true performance of the market, because most are invested in it and government and banks manipulate it. As crazy as it sounds, some are still using those false numbers of the 1980s and 1990s to sell the idea of how wealthy the market will make you.

You may question my use of the words "false numbers," because if you look at market numbers those huge returns really did happen. However, today that is not the case. There are 10,000 baby boomers a day retiring and pulling money out, as well as a large percent of the population who do not want in. For these reasons, the market is not getting those same RORs. As you see in Chart 7-1 on page 26, in the last 19 years the average ROR has been 5.6-7.6 percent. That is a long way from the averages of 12 and 15 percent seen in the 1980s.

CHART 7-1

First Year: 2000	Present Value: 1		Annual Payment
Last Year: 2019	DJ-NoDiv	S&P-NoDiv	S&P-Div	DJ-Bond

AVERAGE ROR:	5.76%	5.60%	7.63%
ACTUAL ROR:	4.77% *	4.02% *	6.04% *
Year	Dow Jones Ind. NO Dividends	S&P 500 NO Dividends	S&P 500 With Dividends
2000	(6.26)	(10.14)	(9.07)
2001	(5.38)	(13.04)	(11.85)
2002	(14.55)	(23.37)	(21.98)
2003	20.94	26.38	28.45
2004	3.07	8.99	10.87
2005	1.10	3.00	4.92
2006	15.00	13.62	15.68
2007	4.56	3.53	5.51
2008	(30.74)	(38.49)	(36.63)
2009	17.15	23.45	25.85
2010	10.27	12.78	14.89
2011	6.23	(0.00)	2.23
2012	8.19	13.41	16.00
2013	22.58	29.60	32.23
2014	8.46	11.39	13.63
2015	(3.84)	(0.73)	1.46
2016	15.94	9.54	11.85
2017	24.86	19.42	21.64
2018	(5.95)	(6.24)	(4.28)
2019	23.66	28.88	31.29

RATES OF RETURN

So many of us hear the term "average rate of return," but what does that really mean? It's important to understand because that is how you are sold on these retirement scams.

There are two types of returns - **average rates of return and actual rates of return**. You must understand the difference because it drastically affects your bottom line.

What the Chart 7-2 on the next page is saying is if you put $1,000 in an account at the beginning of Year One and your investment lost 50 percent that year, then you ended the year with $500. You then begin Year Two with that new balance of $500 and this year's investment earned 100 percent to bring your account balance back up to $1,000. In Year Three your beginning balance is $1,000 and again your investment loses 50 percent, so you are back down to $500. Finally, in Year Four you begin with the $500 balance but make 100 percent again and you end with the same $1,000 you started with.

CHART 7-2

Year	Acct Beginning Balance	Percentage Acct Increased	Ending Acct Balance
1	$1,000	(50%)	$500
2	$500	100%	$1,000
3	$1,000	(50%)	$500
4	$500	100%	$1,000
	Average ROR: 25% Actual ROR: 0%		

Your investment statement and advisor would say this an average rate of return of 25 percent. You walk away feeling great and that is a true statement. However, did you make money? NO. You started with a $1,000 and you ended with $1,000. **The actual rate of return is 0 percent!** Does the average matter here when you didn't make any money over this four-year period of time? No. It's not the average rate of return that matters, **it's the actual rate of return that is more important.** It's like saying your hair is on fire and your feet are in a bucket of water so on average you are comfortable.

HANG IN THERE, IT'LL RECOVER

Oh, I remember 2008-2009 like it was yesterday. I remember calling my financial advisor and telling her to stop my contributions. Of course, her response was to hang in there and that now is the time to be buying. Buy with what? I was the normal American who didn't understand the market. I was not sitting on a ton of savings waiting to buy!

Then she said, "It'll come back, just stay in for the long haul." Wait, why would I stay in something that guaranteed me nothing? This is the interruption I talked about in an earlier chapter. Your account dropped, and you are now starting to earn from a lower value.

It doesn't matter at what point in life this money is interrupted, you will end up with the same amount at the end of the day.

Chart 7-3 below shows the impact of interrupted growth at different times within 10 years. What you are seeing is that 4 percent uninterrupted will outperform a 6 percent that has been interrupted, and regardless if it happened in year one, five, or 10, the end result was the same. If you hang in there, you may get some returns, but then another interruption comes and you are starting over. What you don't know is when the interruptions will come. Will you have time to recover, or will it happen during retirement when there is no time?

CHART 7-3

Year		Guaranteed Value		Market Loss Yr 10		Market Loss Yr 5		Market Loss Yr 1
		$10,000		$10,000		$10,000		$10,000
1	4%	$10,400	6%	$10,600	6%	$10,600	-20%	$8,000
2	4%	$10,816	6%	$11,236	6%	$11,236	6%	$8,480
3	4%	$11,249	6%	$11,910	6%	$11,910	6%	$8,989
4	4%	$11,699	6%	$12,625	6%	$12,625	6%	$9,528
5	4%	$12,167	6%	$13,382	-20%	$10,100	6%	$10,100
6	4%	$12,653	6%	$14,185	6%	$10,706	6%	$10,706
7	4%	$13,159	6%	$15,036	6%	$11,348	6%	$11,348
8	4%	$13,686	6%	$15,938	6%	$12,029	6%	$12,029
9	4%	$14,233	6%	$16,895	6%	$12,751	6%	$12,751
10	4%	$14,802	-20%	$13,516	6%	$13,516	6%	$13,516

If you lose you should know what you'll need for gains in order to get back to the starting point. Table 7-4 below is a good indicator of what is needed for declines and gains to break even. As you can see, the larger the loss, the bigger the gain must be.

CHART 7-4

AMOUNT OF MARKET DECLINE	GAIN NEEDED TO BREAK EVEN
-5%	5.3%
-10%	11.1%
-25%	33.3%
-33.3%	50%
50%	100%
75%	300%

I have many clients who have numbers to prove what they lost in 2008-2009 was only recovered around 2018-2019! These are the clients who were not contributing money to their investments. You cannot take those contributions into effect when looking for a recovery ROR. And the recovery came just in time for another crash in April 2020, only to start over again.

I do not understand why people accept this as okay, just because you are told it's okay. It is NOT okay, and never has been in my eyes.

MANAGEMENT FEES

You are finally hearing about management fees for investment accounts. In fact, it's now mandatory that all fee paperwork is sent to you in order for you to know what those fees are. It doesn't mean they make it easy to understand. But they can legally say it was sent. I do believe this change was due to a PBS Frontline show called *The Retirement Gamble* that aired in 2013. I highly suggest you track it down and watch it.

The **actual** rate of return we looked at earlier had not even factored in the fees. Many accounts have charges for expense ratio, transaction costs, cash drag, and tax costs. The true cost of all of these things is 3 to 4 percent! If you don't believe me, do a Google search on "the real cost of owning a mutual fund" and read the Forbes magazine article on it. Those who are paying attention to their accounts are beginning to make noise and expose the truths. If you look back at the actual ROR of 4 percent in the last 19 years and add in the fees of 3 percent, the account made 1 percent. Do you see what is wrong with this picture?

To show the impact of these fees I am using the Qualified Plan calculator from Truth Concepts. There is nothing exclusive about these calculators to our industry, you yourself can get this same calculator by going to *www.truthconcepts.com*.

What you see in Chart 7-5 on the next page is an individual who is 30 years old and contributing $5,000 a year to a 401k until age 65. There is a rate of return of 4 percent, meaning never a loss in the market. Steady 4 percent every year. You see the retirement Net Account Value is $403,511.

Now take a look at the calculation on Chart 7-6 on page 32 and see what happens to that same account if you add a 2 percent Management Fee. There is a loss of $87,668. That is a 22 percent loss to fees and a 35 percent actual account loss. The account loss is due to the fact that the $87,668 was not in your account growing. And this is only a 2 percent management fee effect.

CHART 7-5

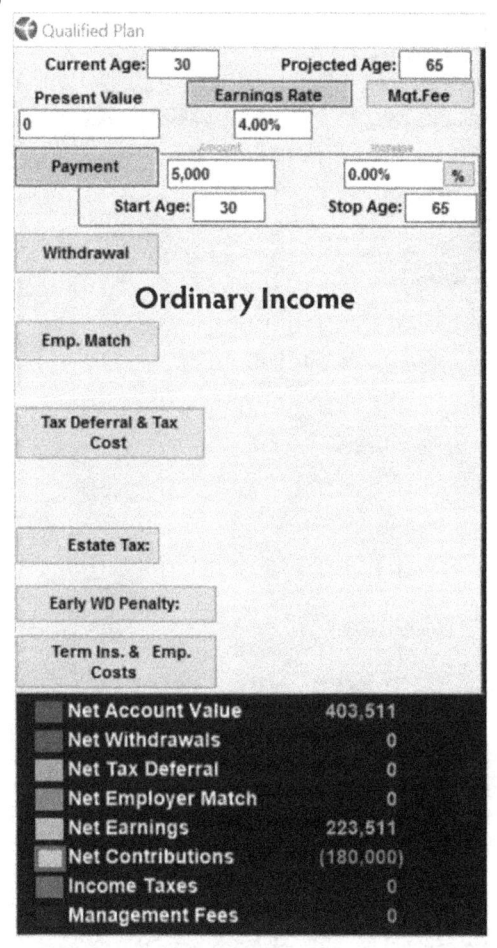

Qualified Plan		
Current Age: 30	Projected Age: 65	
Present Value	Earnings Rate	Mgt.Fee
0	4.00%	
Payment	Amount 5,000	Increase 0.00% %
Start Age: 30	Stop Age: 65	

Withdrawal

Ordinary Income

Emp. Match

Tax Deferral & Tax Cost

Estate Tax:

Early WD Penalty:

Term Ins. & Emp. Costs

Net Account Value	403,511
Net Withdrawals	0
Net Tax Deferral	0
Net Employer Match	0
Net Earnings	223,511
Net Contributions	(180,000)
Income Taxes	0
Management Fees	0

What if it was more realistic at 3 or 4 percent as I indicated above? Look at Chart 7-7 and 7-8 on page 33 to see what a 3 and 4 percent fee looks like. A 3 percent fee would bring that management fee to $115,409, which is a 29 percent loss to fees and a reduction in account value of 47 percent. A 4 percent fee would be $135,977, which is a 34 percent loss to fees and a reduction in account value of 57 percent!

CHART 7-6

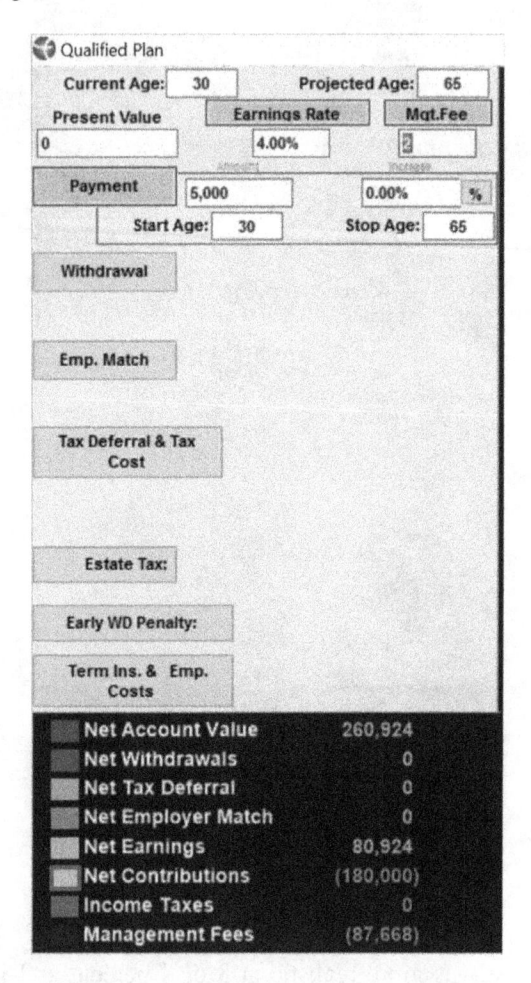

Qualified Plan			
Current Age: 30		Projected Age: 65	
Present Value	Earnings Rate		Mgt.Fee
0	4.00%		
Payment	5,000		0.00% %
Start Age: 30		Stop Age: 65	

Withdrawal

Emp. Match

Tax Deferral & Tax Cost

Estate Tax:

Early WD Penalty:

Term Ins. & Emp. Costs

Net Account Value	260,924
Net Withdrawals	0
Net Tax Deferral	0
Net Employer Match	0
Net Earnings	80,924
Net Contributions	(180,000)
Income Taxes	0
Management Fees	(87,668)

CHART 7-7

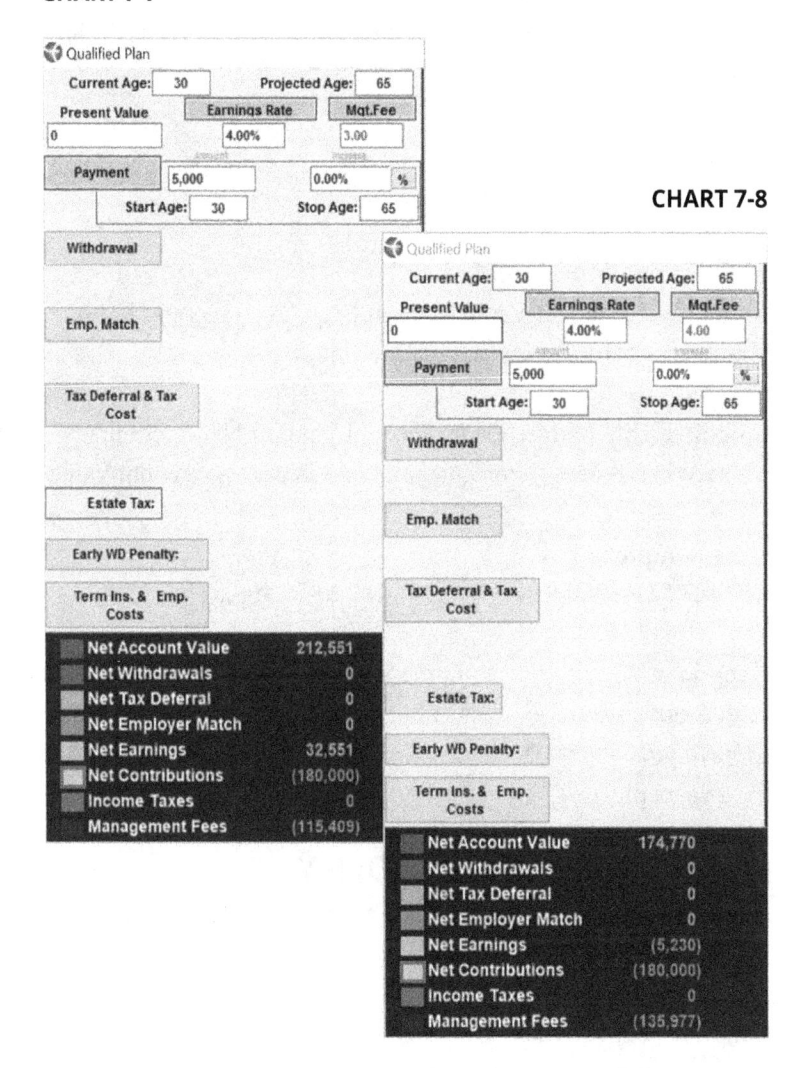

Qualified Plan			
Current Age: 30		Projected Age: 65	
Present Value	Earnings Rate		Mgt.Fee
0	4.00%		3.00
Payment	5,000	0.00%	%
	Start Age: 30	Stop Age: 65	

Withdrawal

Emp. Match

Tax Deferral & Tax Cost

Estate Tax:

Early WD Penalty:

Term Ins. & Emp. Costs

Net Account Value	212,551
Net Withdrawals	0
Net Tax Deferral	0
Net Employer Match	0
Net Earnings	32,551
Net Contributions	(180,000)
Income Taxes	0
Management Fees	(115,409)

CHART 7-8

Qualified Plan			
Current Age: 30		Projected Age: 65	
Present Value	Earnings Rate		Mgt.Fee
0	4.00%		4.00
Payment	5,000	0.00%	%
	Start Age: 30	Stop Age: 65	

Withdrawal

Emp. Match

Tax Deferral & Tax Cost

Estate Tax:

Early WD Penalty:

Term Ins. & Emp. Costs

Net Account Value	174,770
Net Withdrawals	0
Net Tax Deferral	0
Net Employer Match	0
Net Earnings	(5,230)
Net Contributions	(180,000)
Income Taxes	0
Management Fees	(135,977)

THE MATH

It does no good to tell you numbers if we can't prove those numbers, so here is a little math lesson for you related to Charts 7-7 and 7-8 on the next page.

Percentage lost to fees:
Management Fee / Net Account Value Without Fees = % Going to Fees

Example at 2%
$87,668 / $403,511 = 22%

Actual Loss to Account Value:
Step 1: Net Account Value Without Fees - Net Account Value With Fees = Difference in Account Values

Step 2: THEN Difference in Account Values / Net Account Value Without Fees = Percentage of loss in Actual Account Value

Example at 2%
403,511 - 260,924 = 142,587 142,587 / 403,511 = 35%

Keep in mind with these numbers you are looking at long-term effects not short-term. This is fair to say, because you are going to have your money locked up in there long-term, until you are 59½ years old.

FREE MONEY

"But I'm getting free money if I contribute." The 401k match may be the most enticing thing the 401k has to offer, and most people refer to it as "free money." This may be the single hardest thing for people to see past when the subject is approached, it's hard to give up something free.

Looking at the same example on the next page, let's just add an employer match to this 2 percent management fee example and assume the employer is matching half of what the employee contributes.

As you can see in Chart 7-9 below, this individual received $130,462 in "free money." However, more management fees were taken, the new management fees are $131,502. Look at this - your management fees were more than your match, but, thank goodness for them, because they at least took care of some of the fees.

CHART 7-9

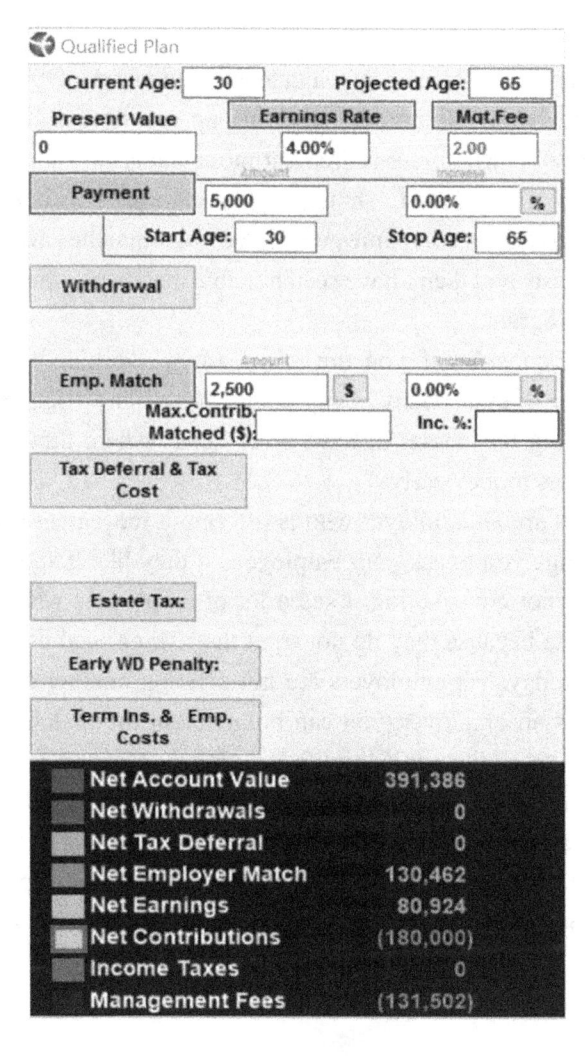

Qualified Plan			
Current Age:	30	Projected Age:	65
Present Value	Earnings Rate		Mgt.Fee
0	4.00%		2.00
Payment	Amount 5,000	Increase 0.00%	%
Start Age:	30	Stop Age:	65
Withdrawal			
Emp. Match	Amount 2,500	$ Increase 0.00%	%
Max.Contrib. Matched ($):		Inc. %:	
Tax Deferral & Tax Cost			
Estate Tax:			
Early WD Penalty:			
Term Ins. & Emp. Costs			

Net Account Value	391,386
Net Withdrawals	0
Net Tax Deferral	0
Net Employer Match	130,462
Net Earnings	80,924
Net Contributions	(180,000)
Income Taxes	0
Management Fees	(131,502)

Look back at all these numbers for their Net Account Value - The account without a match and fees was the best performing account.

> NO Match NO Fees: $403,511
> NO Match With 2 percent Fees: $260,924
> Match With 2 percent Fees: $391,386

What you really need to evaluate is if that match of "free money" is really worth the cost of giving up access to your money (liquidity), putting your retirement money at risk of the market, and subject to a penalty should you need to get to it before age 59½. I have seen companies who have great matches and it may make sense, and then I have seen horrible matches. Dig into your match program.

Also, consider if you are going to be working with that employer forever. Many of my clients have old 401ks, yet they are starting businesses or have other needs where they have to access this money early.

If you are an employer who is offering a retirement account, I challenge you to ask your employees if they like it and/or why they are not contributing. I see a lot of employees who do not contribute because they do not want the risk or need use of that money today. Yet employers are not offering another option to them. As an employer, you can bonus them the match amount and then teach them this Infinite Banking Concept®

I prefer to put my money into a tool that allows me liquidity, control and guarantees. Is there a place you can get a guaranteed rate of return that will not include management fees or penalties and allow your money to remain liquid? Yes, there is. **It's a whole**

life insurance policy with a mutual company structured for liquidity today and retirement tomorrow. You will see how that works in the following chapters.

Should financial advisors get paid to take care of your investment? Yes, they should. Financial advisors are not bad people, just like bankers are not bad people. I have several colleagues who came from the investment world and they had no idea there were fees beyond what they were charging.

However, you should be aware of what those fees are doing to your long-term bottom dollar. Likewise, you should be aware of these same fees that are in the universal, variable and indexed life insurance products.

TAXES AND RETIREMENT

As Americans you are caught up in rates of returns and what your account balance should be at age 65. Many feel $1 million is a great amount of money. Yet a million is not nearly enough to take us through the retirement years to live comfortably.

How much you will have saved at retirement is not nearly as important as how much you will need during retirement. It is critical you find the correct tool to get you as much money as you can for as long as you can during retirement. You must plan for taxes and inflation, which are the silent financial killers.

What is not being taught is how this income from your investment is being taxed at retirement. You put the money in pre-tax, then when you take it out you must pay taxes on it. A great example of this is seed versus harvest. Pretend you garden and you buy a packet of corn seed. If the clerk asks if you want to pay tax on the seed or the harvest, what would you do? Well, one kernel produces around 800 kernels. Knowing this you would quickly pay tax on the seed, because it would be much less than you would pay on the harvest. Yet, you are doing the exact opposite with your invested money - you are deciding to pay on the harvest just to get a tax incentive on the seed.

The tax break is very convincing when you hear you will be in a lower tax bracket at retirement. In fact, many think there are special tax brackets for retirees. There are not. In order to be in a lower tax bracket, you have to either take in less income per year OR taxes must go down. Do you think taxes will go down when those in our government keep printing money and giving handouts? Someone has to pay for this and it won't be them, they don't make money, they only take money.

If you decide to work during retirement, you will have income from your job and possibly some extra income from retirement accounts. This is all income you must claim as ordinary income. This may keep you at the current income level you were at prior to retirement, depending on how much you pull from your retirement account. If that is the case, your income stayed the same, your tax bracket stayed the same or higher, and your deductions decreased, especially if you no longer have a house payment (as the experts suggest) or business deductions if you sold or closed your business.

Everyone I talk to who have been good savers and built their retirement accounts to live comfortably, are paying more taxes during retirement then they did prior to retirement. The only way this works otherwise is to either put money in the correct tool or change your lifestyle by living on less.

It's a bit clearer when you see it laid out. In Chart 7-10 on the next page, there are three "buckets" in which income is taxed. Ordinary Income is taxed at the highest rate, next is Passive Income, and of course the No Income bucket is self-explanatory. The goal at retirement is to have money coming in from the last two buckets and have little to nothing in the Ordinary Income bucket. You want the majority of your money in the No Income tax bucket so you pay less in taxes and live on more.

CHART 7-10

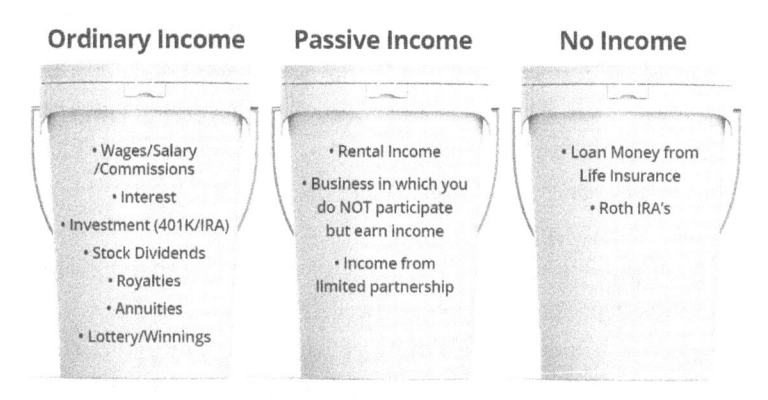

Ordinary Income	Passive Income	No Income
• Wages/Salary/Commissions • Interest • Investment (401K/IRA) • Stock Dividends • Royalties • Annuities • Lottery/Winnings	• Rental Income • Business in which you do NOT participate but earn income • Income from limited partnership	• Loan Money from Life Insurance • Roth IRA's

U.S. Appeals Court Judge Learned Hand said it best, "There are two types of taxation in the country, one for the informed and one for the uninformed." Which type do you want to be?

It does not end there. The good old government has also added another rule to the playbook. You must take the required minimum distribution (RMD) from your investments at age 72 (it used to be 70½). The RMD is a calculated amount you should take out based on a formula. If you do not take this amount, you are slammed with a 50 percent tax of that amount! Regardless if you need it or not, you will take it to avoid the 50 percent tax, which in turn increases ordinary income which increases taxes.

Ponder this for a minute - a 10 percent tax penalty is assumed to withdraw retirement money before age 59½ and then there's another penalty for not using it after age 72. This means there are only 12 1/2 years where your money is not subject to government penalties or requirements.

The other option to reduce taxes is to live on less. If you work today and it takes you $80,000 to live, how will it be less tomorrow when you retire? There is this little thing called inflation, the cost of goods goes up. What is $80,000 today is not buying the same $80,000 in 20 years. You will be forced to downsize and change your living if you are not prepared for inflation and taxes. Retirement should be comfortable, not uncomfortable.

I have run the numbers several times on what it cost 20 years ago for something versus today's cost. There is an average 4 percent inflation. If you just use that number on our $80,000 living expenses over 20 years, you will need $175,290 a year to live like you do today.

When you want to buy a car and pay cash, you put money into a savings account, and you know it is going to be there when you need it. Yet the biggest thing you save for is retirement and, instead of saving that money where you know you will have it, you put it at risk, never really knowing what you will have until the time comes. You plan your retirement on unknowns, not guarantees, and you are taught to believe this is okay.

RETIREMENT DISTRIBUTION

What this all means to you is that you must have enough in your retirement account to cover living expenses, taxes, and inflation. You will most likely need income for 20 to 30 years. Do you know for certain that money will last? What matters most is if you will have enough money to live. The goal should be to live without worry.

On Chart 7-11 on the next page you will see how market ups and downs truly affect you when you are in retirement and taking money out. In this example, you will need to withdraw money for 20 years from the $1 million you have accumulated for retirement. Shown on chart 7-13, you plan to make a 7.63 percent rate of return, because that has been the average of the last 19 years (2000-2019 S&P 500 with dividends). As you can see in the first illustration, if you earn this 7.63 percent and withdraw $80,000 each year you will still have money at the end of 20 years.

CHART 7-11

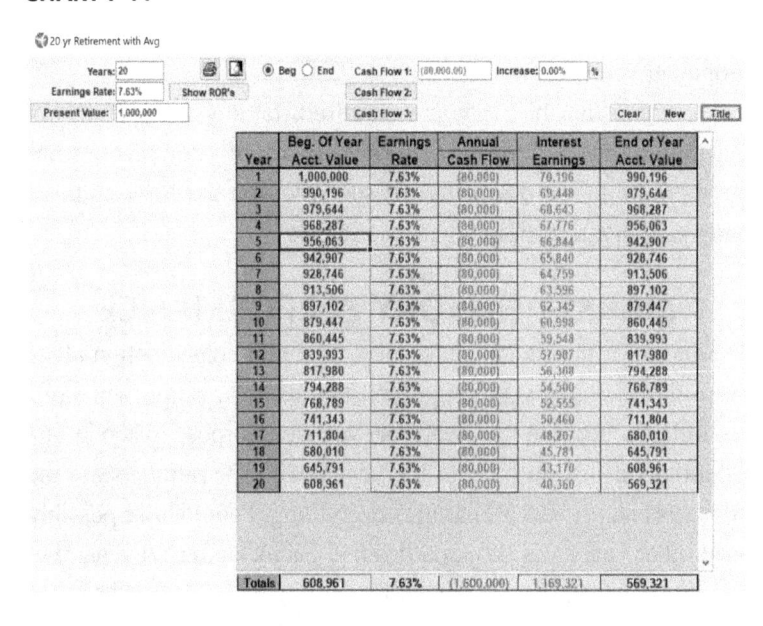

20 yr Retirement with Avg

Years: 20 ● Beg ○ End Cash Flow 1: (80,000.00) Increase: 0.00%
Earnings Rate: 7.63% Show ROR's Cash Flow 2:
Present Value: 1,000,000 Cash Flow 3: Clear New Title

Year	Beg. Of Year Acct. Value	Earnings Rate	Annual Cash Flow	Interest Earnings	End of Year Acct. Value
1	1,000,000	7.63%	(80,000)	70,196	990,196
2	990,196	7.63%	(80,000)	69,448	979,644
3	979,644	7.63%	(80,000)	68,643	968,287
4	968,287	7.63%	(80,000)	67,776	956,063
5	956,063	7.63%	(80,000)	66,844	942,907
6	942,907	7.63%	(80,000)	65,840	928,746
7	928,746	7.63%	(80,000)	64,759	913,506
8	913,506	7.63%	(80,000)	63,596	897,102
9	897,102	7.63%	(80,000)	62,345	879,447
10	879,447	7.63%	(80,000)	60,998	860,445
11	860,445	7.63%	(80,000)	59,548	839,993
12	839,993	7.63%	(80,000)	57,987	817,980
13	817,980	7.63%	(80,000)	56,308	794,288
14	794,288	7.63%	(80,000)	54,500	768,789
15	768,789	7.63%	(80,000)	52,555	741,343
16	741,343	7.63%	(80,000)	50,460	711,804
17	711,804	7.63%	(80,000)	48,207	680,010
18	680,010	7.63%	(80,000)	45,781	645,791
19	645,791	7.63%	(80,000)	43,170	608,961
20	608,961	7.63%	(80,000)	40,360	569,321

| Totals | 608,961 | 7.63% | (1,600,000) | 1,169,321 | 569,321 |

CHART 7-12

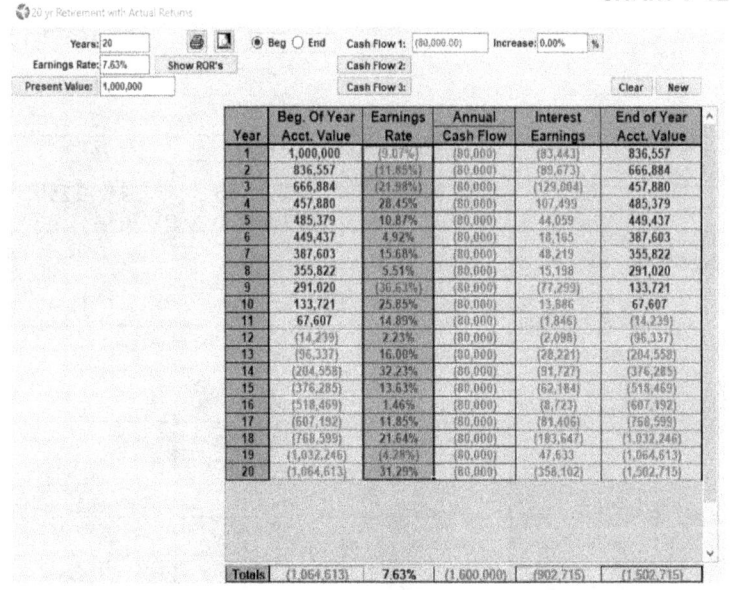

20 yr Retirement with Actual Returns

Years: 20 ● Beg ○ End Cash Flow 1: (80,000.00) Increase: 0.00%
Earnings Rate: 7.63% Show ROR's Cash Flow 2:
Present Value: 1,000,000 Cash Flow 3: Clear New

Year	Beg. Of Year Acct. Value	Earnings Rate	Annual Cash Flow	Interest Earnings	End of Year Acct. Value
1	1,000,000	(9.07%)	(80,000)	(83,443)	836,557
2	836,557	(11.85%)	(80,000)	(89,673)	666,884
3	666,884	(21.98%)	(80,000)	(129,004)	457,880
4	457,880	28.45%	(80,000)	107,499	485,379
5	485,379	10.87%	(80,000)	44,059	449,437
6	449,437	4.92%	(80,000)	18,165	387,603
7	387,603	15.68%	(80,000)	48,219	355,822
8	355,822	5.51%	(80,000)	15,198	291,020
9	291,020	(30.61%)	(80,000)	(77,299)	133,721
10	133,721	25.85%	(80,000)	13,886	67,607
11	67,607	14.89%	(80,000)	(1,846)	(14,239)
12	(14,239)	2.23%	(80,000)	(2,098)	(96,337)
13	(96,337)	16.00%	(80,000)	(28,221)	(204,558)
14	(204,558)	32.23%	(80,000)	(91,727)	(376,285)
15	(376,285)	13.63%	(80,000)	(62,184)	(518,469)
16	(518,469)	1.46%	(80,000)	(8,723)	(607,192)
17	(607,192)	11.85%	(80,000)	(81,406)	(768,599)
18	(768,599)	21.64%	(80,000)	(183,647)	(1,032,246)
19	(1,032,246)	(4.28%)	(80,000)	47,633	(1,064,613)
20	(1,064,613)	31.25%	(80,000)	(358,102)	(1,502,715)

| Totals | (1,064,613) | 7.63% | (1,600,000) | (902,715) | (1,502,715) |

But what happens when you put in the actual rates of return of those years. Below, in Chart 7-12, you end up running out of money at year 12!

How can that be? If you are retired, taking money out, not putting any in, and hit by a market downturn your account has nowhere to go but down. In this scenario you got hit with three bad years in a row right when you retired.

MARKET HISTORY PERFORMANCE

The moral of this story is you must take into consideration all of these factors - taxes, inflation, and market risk. Some will say I am full of it because I picked these years on purpose, when in fact I figured I'd just go back to the year 2000. The numbers are the numbers and prove that timing is everything. I could have possibly used other years and shown a positive balance after 20 years, but do you know what the market will do during your 30 years? No one does and this random selection from Chart 7-13 proves it to be true.

CHART 7-13

Market History

First Year: 2000 Present Value: 0 Annual Payment
Last Year: 2019   DJ-NoDiv | S&P-NoDiv | S&P-Div | DJ-Bond

AVERAGE ROR:	5.76%	5.60%	7.63%
Year	Dow Jones Ind. NO Dividends	S&P 500 NO Dividends	S&P 500 With Dividends
2000	(6.26)	(10.14)	(9.07)
2001	(5.38)	(13.04)	(11.85)
2002	(14.55)	(23.37)	(21.98)
2003	20.94	26.38	28.45
2004	3.07	8.99	10.87
2005	1.10	3.00	4.92
2006	15.00	13.62	15.68
2007	4.56	3.53	5.51
2008	(30.74)	(38.49)	(36.63)
2009	17.15	23.45	25.85
2010	10.27	12.78	14.89
2011	6.23	(0.00)	2.23
2012	8.19	13.41	16.00
2013	22.58	29.60	32.23
2014	8.46	11.39	13.63
2015	(3.84)	(0.73)	1.46
2016	15.94	9.54	11.85
2017	24.86	19.42	21.64
2018	(5.95)	(6.24)	(4.28)
2019	23.66	28.88	31.29

CONTRACT WITH THE GOVERNMENT

With our economy being what it is, many people I talk to wouldn't trust the government with a dollar, yet they do not see the correlation between their investment and the government. If you look back at Rick Beuter's book again, you see that the government was behind the movement for 401ks and IRAs. This simple fact shows us that these pieces of paper are nothing more than a contract with the government.

The government literally makes the rules, and you put up the money. If you don't believe that, ponder this - 401k plans are named after the IRS code 401k. The tax penalty of 10 percent can change at any time as it did in 2010 and during the Covid crisis in 2020. Max contribution limits can change at any time (as they do almost yearly), withdrawal rules change (as they did when the age increased from 70½ to 72), and payback terms are controlled if money is borrowed. You put up the money and take on the risk.

R. Nelson Nash always said if you have plans like this you are in business with the government and he referred to them as government plans. I would agree.

It speaks volumes when Ted Benna, the "father of the 401k," recognizes that it has gotten out of hand. His original intention of looking out for the hard-working American was great. But it did not accomplish that original intention to replace pensions.

Today the hard-working American is being taken advantage of when you look at all the numbers we just discussed in this chapter. The discouraging part is Benna feels it's not good, but it's reality. Sadly, he is correct. The reality is that people don't pay attention and hand over their money for someone else to manage. **Wealth is not built on Wall Street, unless you are the one holding the cards.**

CHAPTER EIGHT

A Better Way to Pay for College

"You learn something every day if you pay attention."
- Ray LeBlond

You have all heard the next bubble to burst will be student loans. Why? Because the cost of tuition is nothing more than a racket and is rising at the rate of 6 percent a year. They can get away with this as long as parents push their kids to go to college.

When I graduated from high school, attending college was a must, and if you didn't go it was almost shameful. I am seeing that change a bit as the cost of tuition is making people rethink whether it's necessary to go and if the job opportunities will be there. Higher pay for jobs with a college degree are not as easy to come by anymore.

Those saving for their kids' college are most likely doing it in a 529 Plan. Yet, this is another great government plan very similar to retirement plans with rules and risk. One rule is your child must go to college or there's a penalty to use this money. Well, best of luck, not all kids are meant to go to college. And, do you really want them going just so they can use this money on beer? I will throw my opinion in here and say, college is not necessary for everyone.

Then there is that pesky little thing called risk. These plans do not have any guaranteed growth. If tuition is increasing by 6 percent, you'd better be earning at least 6 percent a year - with no losses - to ensure there is money for college. We all know that is unlikely since the market tends to crash every 10 years.

What if your children are going to college on Year 10 just in time for the market to crash? This will affect how much money they will have to pay for tuition over the next four years. What if they go to school during that three-year loss we showed from 2000-2003. Would they have enough then or are you digging deep at the last minute to cover it? Again, you are saving in a gambling plan for something you know will require a certain amount of money.

We also hear a lot about or feel guilted into paying for our kids' college. You would never want to saddle your kids with all that debt! Now, as admirable and selfless as it may sound to put your kids through college, it is costing you, the parent, your retirement. Unless of course you just have an overabundance of money or don't plan to retire, then it's no worry. I want to quickly show you on Chart 8-1 on page 46 what the true cost of education looks like and how that will hurt your retirement dollars. Kids, beware, Mom and Dad will be moving in with you.

Please note - I have rounded all numbers below to the nearest thousand.

Let's assume you are a 35-year-old parent, you have kids who are ages six and four, and today's college tuition is $16,000 per year (including books, food and tuition). With a 6 percent tuition increase annually when they go to college, at age 18, tuition will be $32,000 and $36,000 respectively for their first year of college! On top of that, most kids today are going to school for five years, not four.

As a 35-year-old parent today, if you planned to pay for all five years of school for both of your kids, you are looking at a total education cost of $385,000 over a 10-year period of time.

You would have to save nearly $15,600 per year from ages 35 to 53 to pay for this.

On top of that, you the parent could have had this money for retirement. You have an actual asset loss of $718,000, which includes a distribution loss of $42,000 a year from ages 65 to 90. All this is figured on a 4 percent rate of return.

CHART 8-1

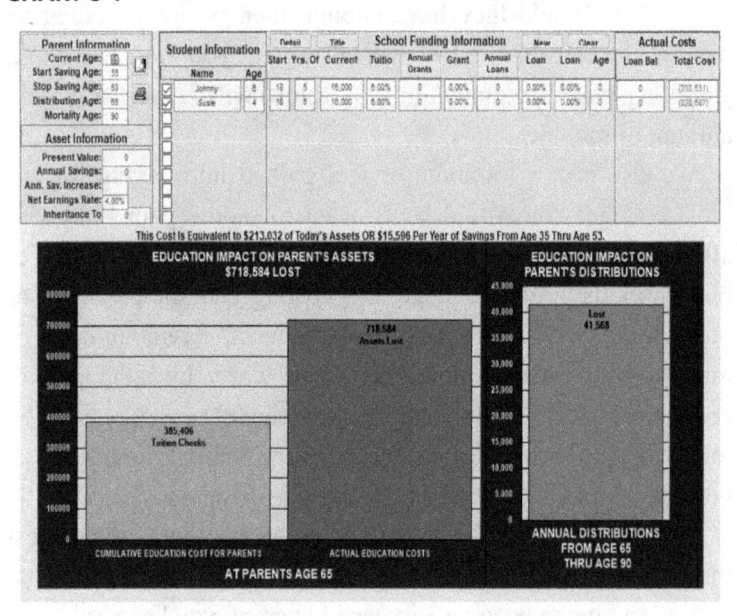

I am not saying don't help your kids through college, please do if you feel that is right. What I am saying is be aware of the true cost. You CAN help your kids through college. It's just a matter of using the right tool and doing it correctly.

CHAPTER NINE

It's All How You Think

"If you change the way you look at things, the things you look at change."
- Wayne Dyer

The first half of this book was sharing a thought process meant to educate you and get you thinking like a banker. This second half is going to outline the tool you need to accomplish all these things and how that works.

Now that your thinking is right and you are educated on the numbers, let's look at the tool that allows you uninterrupted compound interest, along with the control and liquidity you want, all without the risk of the market. The tool is a **properly structured dividend paying whole life insurance policy**.

Life insurance? Yes, a very unlikely tool in today's world. This is where you will find out if you have the arrival syndrome or if you are open minded enough to continue.

The reason is very simple - it is the only tool that allows for all the benefits you are looking for.

1 Uninterrupted compound interest
2 Liquidity
3 Dividends
4 Tax-deferred growth
5 Tax-free retirement when used correctly
6 No market risk

This really does hit all the factors we discussed in prior chapters. I'll break it down briefly here and then dive deeper as we go.

We have talked about the fact that you should own the bank. When you own a whole life insurance policy with a mutual company, you own part of that company. Hence you own the bank. When that company makes a profit, it shares that profit with the owners in the form of a dividend.

We have also talked about you being the banker and having liquid money you can access without question. When you own a whole life policy, it builds a pool of money called cash value. This money is liquid, and you are able to borrow against the cash value and use it without question and without penalty. Hence you are the banker. The next chapter talks more about this.

You also read how important it was to earn uninterrupted compound interest. A whole life insurance policy allows your cash value to grow uninterrupted even while you borrow against that money to make purchases. No other tool allows us this feature, maybe why you never hear about this type of interest.

And finally, taxes. With current retirement vehicles, all that income comes to you as ordinary income - putting you in the highest tax bracket. Remember, you want as much as possible coming to you in the No Income Tax bucket. And, borrowing against your whole life cash value allows this. You will claim no income taxes because it's borrowed money.

A dividend-paying whole life insurance policy is the perfect tool for creating your personal bank, with a death benefit as an added bonus. Truly, you can have a Life Without the Bank!

You may not have heard about whole life insurance or don't understand it, so I do believe a quick background on this is important. It is not new, nor is this idea. This tool and these companies have been around and succeeded for more than 140 years. That is important to recognize when you start comparing it to other things like the Federal Reserve and retirement plans like 401ks and IRAs. The Federal Reserve was formed about 100 years ago - and look at the mess it has created with the devaluation of our dollar. Current retirement plans have been around for about 45 years and are not as traditional nor proven as something 140 years old.

The insurance companies are not allowed to turn money like the banks, which turn every dollar into 10. If you look back you'll see that pensions were put into life insurance products and were guaranteed to be paid out. Agree with pensions or not, the tool used was guaranteed and it worked. I feel the perfect question would be, "Why did we stop using these products and who is benefiting by the change?"

Another important feature is whole life insurance is a contract between you and the insurance company. When you own that contract you have first right to access the cash value. The insurance company cannot make changes - once the premium is set, it is set. There are guarantees which the company must meet. In this case you've both agreed to the terms, no one is taking risk over the other.

WHOLE LIFE VERSUS OTHER PERMANENT PRODUCTS

As we talk about whole life, **don't be confused** with today's other popular permanent products such as Universal, Variable, Flexible Universal, Variable Universal and Equity Indexed, which also have cash value. Agents often call and sell them as whole life, but **they are nothing like whole life**.

There are only two types of insurance, term and permanent. Permanent is meant to provide coverage until death. Under this umbrella falls whole life along with the others mentioned above. Just because someone is talking about cash value doesn't mean they have the right product. Terminology is very important here! It happens nearly daily that new clients say they have whole life and instead have one of these other policies.

Whole life is not based on market returns or performance while the others are. This is why whole life is the only tool used for the Infinite Banking Concept®. Here are just a few big reasons why universal, variable, and indexed are not to be used:

1 Company profits go to the shareholders of the insurance company rather than the policy owners. NO dividends.

2 Cash value and death benefit are in a position where they can be affected by the markets' fluctuations.

3 Some have guarantees to never drop below zero if the market goes negative. Yet fees are taken from the policy each year, which means you went negative because of policy fees being charged to you.

4 Cash value has a surrender period and charge, which means not all the money is accessible for you to borrow against or even get back should you decide to cancel within the period.

5 Policy illustrations are typically run on assumptions of market returns. This tends to lead to underfunding policy premiums where you then see a policy collapse around 70 years old.

> *Get more information by listening to Mary Jo's podcast, Without the Bank.*

CHART 9-1

Policy Information

Owner:		Policy Date:	April 27, 2009
Insured:		Gender:	Female
Issue Age: 64		Risk Class:	Non-Tobacco Plus Non-Tobacco

Summary of Current Coverage

Face Amount:	$500,000.00	Annual Planned Premium:	$11,300.04
Current Death Benefit:	$500,000.00	Planned Premium Frequency:	Monthly
Additional Agreements:		Billing Method:	EFT
Death Benefit Guarantee Agreement		Death Benefit Option:	Level
Overloan Protection Agreement		Death Benefit Qualification Test:	
		Guideline Premium Test	

Accumulation Value Summary

Accumulation Value on 04/27/2013:	$23,692.07	Accumulation Value on 04/27/2014:	$28,960.39
Premiums Received:	$11,300.04	**Surrender Charge**	$-15,924.72
Net Investment Gain/Loss**	$772.00	Surrender Value	$13,035.67
Premium Charges	$-452.04		
Cost of Insurance Charges	$-3,868.36		
Total Monthly Policy Charges	$-96.00		
Policy Issue Charges	$-2,274.96		
M & E Risk Charges	$-93.45		
Additional Agreements Charges	$-18.91		
Accumulation Value on 04/27/2014:	$28,960.39		

**May include unrealized loan interest credit.

Chart 9-1 is an image of a client's Variable Universal Life policy. I have included this (with permission) to show you what happens with charges/fees inside policies of this kind. As you can see, his premium per year is $11,300 for $500,000 of death benefit. Then you take a look at the Accumulation Value Summary section, which shows there are charges for Cost of Insurance, Premium Charges, Monthly Policy Charges, Policy Issues Charges, M&E (Mortality) Risk Charges and Additional Agreements Charges. If you add all these charges up, **he is paying $6,803 a year in charges. That means 60 percent of his premium is going to charges.**

None of these are set charges - they fluctuate every year. The Cost of Insurance Charge is based on the current age of the insured. As the insured gets older, this charge gets higher, because the insured is more likely to die and the company anticipates having to pay. It's like having a term policy that renews every year at your new age.

It gets worse. Look over at Chart 9-1, you see Accumulation Value as of 04/27/2014, Surrender Charge and Surrender Value. What this is saying is he has a total cash value of $28,960, but if he decides to cancel the policy he will only get the $13,035. The company is going to keep the rest as a Surrender Charge. Even if he wanted to borrow against this money, he still only has access to the $13,035.

If you look at the rate of return in this policy, there was a **-17.24 percent rate of return**, and this was in a year when the market was supposed to be doing well. Yes, there was an increase in accumulation, but there was also a contribution of $11,300. Had he not contributed, the loss would have been even greater.

The end result here is most likely not going to be good. With a -17 percent return this means the policy owner was not paying enough premium (underfunded policy) to make up the difference that was lost due to these charges and fees. What happens at this point is the company will take money from cash value to make up the difference! Yes, it takes it without notification! This continues each year as the charges increase and premium continues to be too low. At some point the cash value will run out and the policy will lapse, or the policy owner will have to come up with some huge increased premium.

Look at your policies. The majority of the time the policy illustration or yearly statement will indicate when this policy will terminate. If it is before age 85, you may clearly outlive the policy. You paid a premium with an intention to use it at retirement or have the death benefit for your heirs, and you may not have either. This is not intended to be a "the world is falling" scenario, rather it's an opportunity for you be aware and prepare. I've seen them lapse at age 50!

The next logical question is, "Why are these types of policies even sold?" My thoughts on the matter are these - insurance companies came up with these products to compete with the market growth in the 1980s as people were dumping their whole life policies for a better rate of return. This was a big mistake by the insurance industry, because slow and steady wins the race.

Then you have the financial gurus of today pushing these policies because that is what they are taught to do. But many of them do not have a clue what they are doing and why. And finally, people buy death benefit based on price because that is what they have been taught to do. These universal, variable, and indexed products are typically underfunded (cheaper premium) because the market gain is supposed to make up the difference that's not being paid for.

In a whole life insurance policy, you do not have these charges that come out of your pocket, an underfunded premium nor do you have a surrender charge or period.

You need to build a banking system with a product that will give you the guarantees and has the stability of 140 years behind it. At the end of the day, if you are wanting to implement the Infinite Banking Concept®, you want to only use dividend paying whole life. There is a reason R. Nelson Nash only sold whole life in the 35 years he was an agent.

TERM INSURANCE

You most likely know more about term insurance, because it is a fairly inexpensive option for death benefit. Term insurance fills only one need, which is death benefit. The misconception is that term insurance is "cheap," which is true until you reach age 66 when premiums increase. What you do not hear is at age 65, coverage that was once around $990 a year is now $15,745 a year for the same coverage, if you remain insurable and are in standard health. The main reason you do not hear this is because you are told you should not need it, because you will have no debt after age 65. This is not even close to a true statement for most, who are often still carrying debt and buying things after age 65.

If you need proof, let's compare the two to tell the whole story. Below are breakdowns of a $500,000 death benefit term policy and a whole life policy. The insured is a 40-year-old male who was rated preferred for the first 30-year term and standard at age 71 for the next 15-year term. If we are going to compare, we need to compare as long as we can and term can only be purchased up to age 85, even though whole life goes to age 121.

CHART 9-2

Age 40-85	Term			Whole Life (numbers illustrated are end of year 10, 20, 30 and 45)		
Policy Year	Yearly Premium	Cash Value	Death Benefit	Yearly Premium	Cash Value	Death Benefit
1-10	$990.00	0	$500,000	$6,485	$58,198	$507,530
11-20	$990.00	0	$500,000	$6,485	$173,977	$560,594
21-30	$990.00	0	$500,000	$6,485	$361,844	$685,291
31-45	$15,745	0	$500,000	$6,485	$843,930	$1,036,341
Total Premium	$265,875			$291,825		

There are a couple things to note from this Chart 9-2:

1 The out-of-pocket premiums are a bit less on the term side. Keep in mind this could change depending on when that second or third term is purchased.

2 The cost of death benefit is far less in the whole life policy than the term policy at age 85, when a male is most likely to pass. In the term policy, the death benefit cost was $0.51 for every dollar, where the whole life was $0.28 for every dollar. If you are buying life insurance, you are buying it for death benefit, so you must figure the true cost of the death benefit upon the likely age one would pass. Term is nearly double and only 1 to 2 percent of term ever pays out.

3 There is no cash value in the term policy, since term does not have cash value. In the whole life policy, you can see there was $843,930 of cash value at age 85. That is far more cash value than you paid in for premium. That is a significant amount of cash value, and please note this policy illustration was NOT structured to be cash value rich, as you do with the Infinite Banking Concept®.

4 Buy term and invest the difference may be running through your head. As you can see in Chart 9-3, the alternate account would have to earn 9.95 percent with management fees of 2 percent and a 25 percent tax to match the whole life insurance policy. That is 9.95 percent every single year for 45 years. No losses. As you see earlier, the market average in the last 20 years is nowhere near this.

CHART 9-3

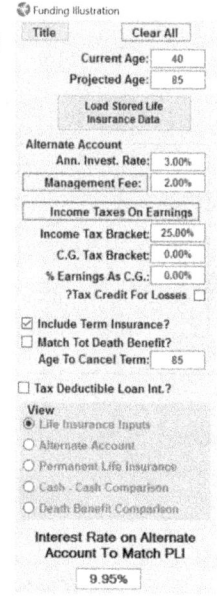

Funding Illustration

Title	Clear All
Current Age:	40
Projected Age:	85

Load Stored Life Insurance Data

Alternate Account
Ann. Invest. Rate:	3.00%
Management Fee:	2.00%

Income Taxes On Earnings
Income Tax Bracket:	25.00%
C.G. Tax Bracket:	0.00%
% Earnings As C.G.:	0.00%
?Tax Credit For Losses	☐

☑ Include Term Insurance?
☐ Match Tot Death Benefit?
Age To Cancel Term: 85

☐ Tax Deductible Loan Int.?

View
● Life Insurance Inputs
○ Alternate Account
○ Permanent Life Insurance
○ Cash - Cash Comparison
○ Death Benefit Comparison

Interest Rate on Alternate Account To Match PLI

9.95%

So the question is, is term really cheaper than whole life in the long run? The answer is no. Term has its place in the market, but it's not the best option for the **long term**.

As R. Nelson Nash says, don't buy life insurance like you're shopping at Wal-Mart.

> ### ACTION STEP:
> *Mary Jo is a certified IBC practitioner and life insurance agent who can help you with this process. Schedule an appointment today and get help from an expert.*

CHAPTER TEN

Cash Surrender Value

"Tell me and I forget. Teach me and I remember. Involve me and I learn."
- Benjamin Franklin

As R. Nelson Nash says, "How many times do you die? Once. Your need for financing in life is greater than your need for a death benefit." Who better to finance your purchases than you?

Even if you are familiar with cash surrender value (which I will refer to going forward as cash value), this chapter is one of the most important. Cash surrender value is the cash value in the policy that you, the policy owner, is allowed to borrow against and use.

Cash value is there for three reasons:

1 If you should decide to cancel (terminate) the policy, the company will send you the amount you have in cash surrender value.

2 It is the amount you can borrow against should you want to take a loan.

3 It is the amount that can also be withdrawn from the policy while the policy remains in effect.

ACCESS TO CASH VALUE

When you pay a premium, some of these premium dollars are accessible through the cash value portion of the policy. With each premium payment cash value increases.

Cash value is your money. You have total access to it for whatever you want, whenever you want it, you have first right to use this money. It is easy to access. When you want a loan, you call your agent, sign a service request form, send it to the life insurance company, and the company sends you the money. Some companies now allow you to go online and request it.

You then decide when and how you will pay it back. It's your loan, and it's your decision. If you want to pay it back in a year's time, you can do that, or pay it back in 10 years' time. The decision is yours, because you are in charge. The only thing you need to remember is it's your account, and you need to be an honest banker and pay it back. If you don't, you stole!

BORROWING AGAINST CASH VALUE

It may sound like a simple process of borrowing and paying back, but you must understand what is going on with your money while you **borrow against** it. Notice how I keep saying borrowing against the cash value. That is for a reason.

When you borrow against your cash value, the life insurance companies leaves your money in your account and uses it as collateral while they lend you their money. They charge you an interest rate to use their money. Key here is **while you are using their money, they continue to pay you uninterrupted compound interest on your money, because it was never removed from your account, just collateralized**. To see this in action, visit my website *www.withoutthebank.com/howitworks*

This is the reason you want to use whole life as your banking tool. It earns uninterrupted compound interest while you leverage your dollar by using the life insurance companies' dollar.

Why doesn't the company care when it is paid back? Because it uses the death benefit and/or the cash value as collateral to the loan. Should you pass away with a loan on your policy, your heirs will get the death benefit minus any loan. This is similar to using your home as collateral to a bank loan. The difference is you are no longer putting your assets (example: home/auto/property/business/etc.) up as collateral. Instead, you are using your death benefit and/or cash value as collateral.

This is a very secure loan for you, because no one is going to take your assets should you become unemployed or disabled and unable to make payments. That is part of what makes this the perfect financial tool for you in good and bad years. It will get you through because you are in control. The fear of the worst-case scenario is now taken care of.

You do however, need to pay the loan back. This is not free money and why it's important to be an honest banker. You would never skip a bank payment so don't skip a loan repayment to your policy.

Keep in mind these are the basics of the process because I can't cover every single loan aspect in this book. You will learn the strategies that work with you should you decide to call and/or work with me on setting up a policy for yourself.

DIVIDENDS

Dividends are a share of the profit from the company and classified as a return of premium by the IRS so they are not taxed. It is imperative to use a mutual company that pays dividends. As we talked about earlier, you want to own the bank so you can receive part of those profits. The dividends are typically put right back into the policy for continued growth but can be paid out to you. Should you have them paid out they are not taxable. Dividends are looked at as a return of premium.

These dividends can become quite large as the years go by, which allows for better growth long term. Dividends are not part of the guarantees, but they have been paid for over 140 years, so I don't feel there is a reason to believe they will stop.

CHAPTER ELEVEN

Protection

"Minds are like flowers, they only open when the time is right."
- Stephen Richards

Even though our need for financing is important, you must not forget that the death benefit is also necessary for our loved ones.

As we discussed earlier, whole life insurance provides coverage up to age 121 (used to be 100). Death benefits are truly an added bonus, not just because they take care of any loan debt in the policy but because your family needs to be taken care of when you are gone.

MORE THAN COLLATERAL

Many say they don't need to leave their family rich, all they need is enough to cover a funeral. I am going to call your bluff on that and tell you to reevaluate your thought process. I had a friend who lost her husband in an accident and, at that point, I realized it was not about making anyone rich but allowing the surviving heirs time to mourn. Have you ever thought of how much time you need to mourn before you have to get back to work and face the world again? How your children will need you to help them through a loss of a parent? Think about it, you don't just get up the next day as if nothing happened. Take a minute and think about what you'd do if your loved one passed tomorrow. How would you handle that? Even those who have time to prepare will tell you they were not prepared.

Another line I hear a lot is, "I need more coverage because I am the working spouse or make more money." What? If you have young kids at home are you telling me you can just up and go to work and do what you do every day should the other spouse be gone? There is no way you would be able to generate the same amount of income taking on everything. And, don't tell me Grandma will take care of the kids. It is not Grandma's job.

It is not easy losing loved ones, and while you were here on earth you were taking care of them. You should at least care enough about them to be sure they are taken care of after you pass.

KEY-MAN POLICY

Insurance is not just for family, it is also a necessary tool to use in business. A key-man policy is a policy you own on other person's lives because you have an insurable interest in them. Insurable interest must constitute some sort of financial loss when that person passes.

Examples of this would be a business partner, a key employee, family whose estate or business you will take over, or children to whom you may have lent money, just to name a few.

It is very common for me to see term insurance key-man policies on business partners. This is great but it should be whole life as soon as the business can afford it. I have seen successful businesses whose partners' term insurance expires and the partner is no longer insurable. Insurance is still needed, yet one of the partners will get nothing upon the death of the other. This leaves the living partner no way to buy out the others' portions upon their death. Another reason is if partnerships go south and you still need the death benefit to make you whole financially. I have seen this happen firsthand. Remember, it's a contract between you and the insurance company, no one can change it.

You cannot just insure others without them knowing. The insured must agree, have a medical exam, answer financial questions and sign off on everything. If you do not have their blessing you are not able to insure them.

Many feel that taking a policy out on another's life is greedy. It is not greedy, it is merely a necessity to keep someone or a business financially whole. Think about it, if you have built a business with someone and they pass, you could lose the business. Why work so hard to build something if you chose not to protect it? No one ever wants to use that policy, yet we are all guaranteed one thing, to die.

It is not uncommon for families and business partners to get into a financial war at times of death. There is nothing that will separate people faster than money issues. Being prepared can be an important way to keep people together.

ACTION STEP:

Mary Jo will go over this in more detail when you schedule your free consultation with her. Check your email or call the office to get scheduled. 701-751-3917

CHAPTER TWELVE

Policy Understanding

"Don't fear that which you don't understand; be curious."
- Matthew Fryer

Before you go any further, it is important to understand the basics of how to read a whole life insurance illustration.

An illustration is nothing more than a projection or outlook of what your policy will look like in the future. In Chart 12-1 on page 64 you will see there are several columns, so let's go over them in detail.

GUARANTEED AND NON-GUARANTEED ASSUMPTIONS COLUMNS

First, there are two sides, guaranteed and non-guaranteed. The Guaranteed side means, by contract, the company will guarantee you will have the illustrated amount of cash value and death benefit shown from interest earned.

The Non-Guaranteed Assumptions side figures in anticipated dividends. Dividends are not something companies can guarantee, but remember, they have successfully paid dividends for more than a century.

CONTRACT PREMIUM

Contract Premium is the amount of premium you have agreed to pay for life insurance each year for the life of the contract. This will never increase, and there are restrictions to decrease it.

It is very important to make sure you are comfortable with this amount from the beginning, because you can only decrease, never increase, the premium.

NET CASH VALUE

Net Cash Value is the amount of money you are able to borrow against or receive should you surrender your policy. You will notice there are two columns for cash value. The Non-Guaranteed side includes the dividends, whereas the Guaranteed side does not.

DEATH BENEFIT

Death Benefit is the amount of money your beneficiaries will receive when you die. Again, there are two columns: Non-Guaranteed includes the death benefit with dividends being paid. Guaranteed does not.

CHART 12-1

			Guaranteed	
Age	Year	Contract Premium	Net Cash Value	Death Benefit
36	1	12,000	7,818	841,361
37	2	12,000	15,946	882,662
38	3	12,000	26,091	922,387
39	4	12,000	37,740	960,598
40	5	12,000	49,844	997,360
41	6	12,000	62,406	1,032,727
42	7	12,000	75,432	1,066,757
43	8	12,000	88,929	1,099,508
44	9	12,000	102,896	1,131,035
45	10	12,000	117,344	1,262,393

CUM(ULATIVE) PREMIUM

Cumulative Premium is the total amount of premium you have paid to the life insurance company up to that particular year.

ANNUAL DIVIDEND

Annual Dividend is your anticipated yearly share of the profits from the company, since you are part owner.

INCREASE IN NET CASH VALUE

Increase in Net Cash Value is the amount your net cash value increased at policy year end after premium and dividends (non-guaranteed) were paid.

Throughout the rest of the book when you see case studies, the numbers used will be from the Non-Guaranteed side. Again, with the company's long history of paying dividends, there is no reason to assume dividends will not be paid. Keep this page handy when moving forward, as you may want to reference these terms again.

Non-Guaranteed Assumptions
100% of Current Dividend Scale

Contract Premium	Cum Premium	Annual Dividend	Increase in Net Cash Value	Net Cash Value	Death Benefit
12,000	12,000	130	7,948	7,948	842,075
12,000	24,000	173	8,306	16,254	884,288
12,000	36,000	224	10,381	26,635	925,149
12,000	48,000	275	11,946	38,580	964,705
12,000	60,000	332	12,469	51,049	1,003,027
12,000	72,000	394	13,003	64,052	1,040,175
12,000	84,000	464	12,554	77,606	1,076,227
12,000	96,000	544	14,126	91,732	1,111,260
12,000	108,000	635	14,710	106,442	1,145,351
12,000	120,000	732	15,315	121,757	1,178,554

CHAPTER THIRTEEN

Young Versus Old

"Education is not the learning of facts, but the training of the mind to think."
- Albert Einstein

So many times I hear, "If only I was younger. I am too old to start using this, but it would be good for those young kids." This is a big misconception because cash value grows nearly equally regardless of age. Everyone of all ages uses money on a daily basis, this should be something all people at least consider. Furthermore, when was the last time the bank told you that you are too old to deposit money?

In order to put this misconception to rest, you will see on Chart 13-1 on page 68 we are using the same amount of premium dollars each year for the next 10 years, and the only difference is age: a 35-year-old and 55-year-old. To compare, you really need to look at two columns: Net Cash Value and Death Benefit.

CASH VALUE

In the Cash Value column, take a look at Year One. You can see the 55-year-old actually has more cash value than the 35-year-old. In fact, the 55-year-old has more money in cash value all the way through year nine, at which point the 35-year-old starts to somewhat outperform. The 55-year-old continues to perform equally as well with the cash value all the way to Year 15.

Something else to look at is the "break even" point. This is the point at which the Cumulative Premium equals the Net Cash Value. In BOTH cases that happens at year 10.

The reason for this equal performance is because the older you are the less time you have to accumulate money. The younger you are, the longer you have, which makes the company look long term at how much you will accumulate in cash value compared to your death benefit. All these factors are taken into consideration when building a correctly structured policy.

DEATH BENEFIT

When looking at the Death Benefits, it's a much different picture. At the age of 55, it costs more for insurance, so you have a far less Death Benefit than you would have at 35. However, just 10 years later, the Death Benefit at 70 is still nearly a half million dollars. Should this 55-year-old pass away at year 10, he gifted his family income tax free money on which he paid $0.21 for every dollar. How else are you going to leave your family with this kind of wealth income tax free?

The moral of the story is you are NOT too old to start a policy for banking.

CHART 13-1

Young vs Old Comparison

35 Year Old Year	36 Year Old Age	Premium	Cumulative Premium	Increase in Cash Value	Net Cash Value	Death Benefit
1	36	12,000	12,000	7,952	7,952	856,464
2	37	12,000	24,000	8,311	16,263	898,700
3	38	12,000	36,000	10,467	26,730	939,585
4	39	12,000	48,000	12,089	38,819	979,164
5	40	12,000	60,000	12,618	51,437	1,017,511
6	41	12,000	72,000	13,158	64,595	1,054,684
7	42	12,000	84,000	13,715	78,310	1,090,761
8	43	12,000	96,000	14,293	92,603	1,125,822
9	44	12,000	108,000	14,882	107,485	1,159,942
10	45	12,000	120,000	15,494	122,978	1,193,176

55 Year Old Year	56 Year Old Age	Premium	Cumulative Premium	Increase in Cash Value	Net Cash Value	Death Benefit
1	56	12,000	12,000	8,490	8,490	373,905
2	57	12,000	24,000	9,122	17,613	395,559
3	58	12,000	36,000	11,511	29,124	416,724
4	59	12,000	48,000	11,963	41,087	437,423
5	60	12,000	60,000	12,430	53,517	457,702
6	61	12,000	72,000	12,904	66,420	477,616
7	62	12,000	84,000	13,377	79,797	497,218
8	63	12,000	96,000	13,858	93,655	516,565
9	64	12,000	108,000	14,347	108,002	535,705
10	65	12,000	120,000	14,852	122,854	554,661

POLICIES ON YOUNG CHILDREN

Thinking that a policy will perform better on minor children is another misconception. First you have the obstacle of state guidelines to write insurance on children. In North Dakota and most other states, the child can only have half the death benefit the parents have. To obtain a copy of your state guidelines, check with your state's insurance department. If you are the parent and have $500,000 death benefit, your child can only have a death benefit of $250,000.

It does not take much premium to get a child's death benefit to $250,000. So, when looking at it as a financial tool, a child's policy will not build cash value any faster than an adult's cash value. In fact, it will be much slower, because you can't structure for cash value growth like you can an adult's.

The second obstacle is most companies will only go up to a million dollars of death benefit on a minor. Again, this can be hard if you have a significant amount of money to put in as premium.

This does not mean you should not be starting a policy on your child. In fact, you should absolutely start a policy on your child, just don't expect to put tens of thousands of dollars of premiums into it. I see far too many young people who are uninsurable, uneducated on money, and stuck with bad loans. They should be taught how to avoid the banks and this a great start.

> *As a certified IBC practitioner and life insurance agent, I can help you get started with this process. I have clients all over the U.S. and we meet virtually. Please call or check your email for a link to my calendar and set up your free consultation.*
>
> *Get more information by listening to Mary Jo's podcast, Without the Bank.*

CHAPTER FOURTEEN

Case Studies

"The great aim of education is not knowledge, but action."
- Herbert Spencer

You have all the information you need on being an honest banker. Now you need to see it implemented.

You can use this concept on many levels and will see that in these case studies. Keep your imagination open when reading through this. **This concept can be used for far more than what is presented in these pages because it is infinite.**

When going forward keep in mind, the numbers are all relative. If the premium looks too high for you, then cut it in half or remove a zero. If the premium is not high enough, increase the amounts by adding a zero. All other numbers you'll do the same with and that will give you an idea of what you are looking at. When you have your appointment with me you will see a customized illustration to match your finances. **Everyone starts at different levels. Getting started is what matters.**

Also, remember these illustrations are all correctly structured policies for the goal of using the Infinite Banking Concept® and this concept is not used by 99 percent of agents or financial planners. Not every company allows us to put money to cash value like this.

In the following case study, Chart 14-1, we are going to use Dale and Amy, who are 40 years old, both employed, and they have a son, Jacob, who is 13 at the time they started their policy.

CASE STUDY - USING YOUR LIFE INSURANCE TODAY

(All numbers have been rounded and no interest was added to loans for simplicity reasons)

Dale and Amy make a household income of $250,000 a year. They know they should be saving 10 percent of their income for retirement, so they wanted to start a policy with a premium of $25,000 per year. (Full premium is on Dale for illustration.) They also decided to fund this premium at the full amount until Dale is 65 years old. Both Dale and Amy know this is the maximum premium, yet if they have a bad year and someone loses a job they are able to decrease the premium. If they have more money, they will need to start another one, once a premium is set that is the maximum, anything extra must go into a new policy.

Since they are good savers, Dale and Amy have money in savings and decided to pay this premium in full. As you can see on the next page, when they pay the $25,000 premium, they have an immediate cash value in year one of $16,701. They can borrow against this money in 10 to 30 days for whatever they want without question!

They decide not to borrow anything until Year Two when Dale upgrades his boat. He requests a $30,000 loan against his cash value to buy his new boat and decides to pay this back as quickly as possible. They are looking for a little house to buy as a rental property for Jacob when he goes off to college. Instead of making monthly loan payments back to the policy Dale is going to use bonus money. Either option would work for him, and if he doesn't get the bonus, it will just slow down the plans **he has for repayment**. He is now acting as his own banker. Bonuses were good and Dale had $10,000 to pay down the loan by the end of the year.

It's now the beginning of Year Three, and he paid his premium, which has increased his cash value available by $23,942 ($58,070 from $34,128). He now has $38,070 to borrow against should he need that money. Again, he receives a bonus of $10,000 and uses that to make is second loan payment.

Year Four comes and he pays his premium, increasing his available cash value by $25,506 and giving him access to a total cash value of $73,576. Now Dale only has $10,000 left on his loan for the year. This year his bonus was not what it had been, and he only had $6,000 to apply to his loan. No big deal, he only has to answer to himself.

Year Five arrives, and he pays his premium and again his cash value increased, this time by $26,525. He only has $4,000 left on his boat loan, and he has access to $106,101. By the end of the year he had enough of a bonus to pay off this loan and now has access to all of his cash value.

It's Year Six. Jacob is now 18 and will be ready for college in the fall. Dale and Amy have been looking for a house to buy, and now is the time. They find a little home for $130,000. They decide to put the $50,000 down and do a 30-year mortgage at 5 percent on the other $80,000 for this home.

They also decided to put Jacob's name on the loan to help him build credit. If they were thinking like the conditioned American, they would think they only have a monthly house payment of $430 because they only financed $80,000 with the bank. However, they borrowed against their cash value for the other $50,000, so their payment should also include the payback of this loan. The typical student is in college five years, so Dale and Amy have figured they would like this down payment amount to be paid back in a six-year time frame. In six years Jacob most likely won't be in this house.

Paying this back over six years increases the monthly mortgage by $805. So they charge Jacob and his friends $1,235 a month for rent.

By the end of the Year Six, Jacob and his roommates have paid back $4,830 of the loan after renting for six months. As you

CHART 14-1

Age	Year	Premium	Cumulative Premium	Increase in Net Cash Value	Net Cash Value	Loan Amt Beg Year	Available Cash Value Beg Year	Loan Repayment	Available CV End Year	Death Benefit
41	1	25,000	25,000	16,701	16,701		16,701			1,068,076
42	2	25,000	50,000	17,427	34,128	-30,000	4,128	10,000	14,128	1,131,116
43	3	25,000	75,000	23,942	58,070	-20,000	38,070	10,000	48,070	1,192,566
44	4	25,000	100,000	25,506	83,576	-10,000	73,576	6,000	79,576	1,252,529
45	5	25,000	125,000	26,525	110,101	-4,000	106,101	4,000	110,101	1,311,135
46	6	25,000	150,000	27,599	137,700	-50,000	87,700	4,830	13,600	1,368,575
47	7	25,000	175,000	28,714	166,414	-45,170	121,244	9,660	130,904	1,424,973
48	8	25,000	200,000	29,890	196,304	-35,510	160,794	9,660	170,454	1,480,358
49	9	25,000	225,000	31,125	227,430	-25,850	201,580	9,660	211,240	1,534,703
50	10	25,000	250,000	32,404	259,834	-16,190	243,644	9,660	253,304	1,588,008
51	11	25,000	275,000	33,709	293,543	-6530	287,013	6,530	293,543	1,640,371
52	12	25,000	300,000	35,054	328,597					1,691,914
53	13	25,000	325,000	36,420	365,017					1,742,758
54	14	25,000	350,000	37,835	402,852					1,793,037
55	15	25,000	375,000	39,261	442,114					1,842,904
56	16	25,000	400,000	40,734	482,848					1,892,518
57	17	25,000	425,000	42,256	525,104					1,941,957
58	18	25,000	450,000	43,844	568,947					1,991,219
59	19	25,000	475,000	45,500	614,447					2,040,261
60	20	25,000	500,000	47,189	661,636					2,089,133
61	21	25,000	525,000	48,881	710,517					2,137,974
62	22	25,000	550,000	50,588	761,105					2,186,970
63	23	25,000	575,000	52,277	813,382					2,236,306
64	24	25,000	600,000	53,984	867,366					2,286,066
65	25	25,000	625,000	55,712	923,077					2,336,248

can see, Dale keeps paying the premium, and Jacob continues to be on time with his rent payments of $9,660 per year until the last year, when he only had $6,530 to pay. Dale is 51 years old, and all his loans are again paid off and he has full cash value of $293,543 available, continuing to be right on track to use that money for retirement.

Let's pause here for a minute and note a couple key points:

1 Look at the Increase in Net Cash Value column. In year four, Dale's cash value increased by $25,506. That cash value increase was a little more than what he paid in premium. The first three years of this policy he did not have access to all his premium dollars. However, by year four, he has access to the same amount he paid in premium that year.

As R. Nelson Nash says in his book, "it takes money to start a business and you don't make a profit right away." This is the same thing. You have to capitalize, and, once the ball is rolling, you're cash value is continuing to increase because of the uninterrupted compound interest and dividends.

Look at Year Five. Cash value increased by $26,525, and Year Seven was $27,599. Keep going down that column. Every year it increases more than the last. Are you okay putting money into a tool that does this, even while you borrow against it?

Many ask how insurance companies can do that without going out of business. It's simple - they have invested their money wisely into bonds and real estate. They have professionally managed portfolios and more than 150 years of profits - even through the 1930s and 2009. I can't speak for all companies, but the companies I represent have very little of their portfolio in the stock market. One of those companies has less than 1 percent of its assets in the market.

This company only lost $300,000 in 2009 out of $20 billion plus in assets, leaving it as number one across the financial market for the least amount lost. This speaks volumes. The company holding your policy better have a good track record of success.

2 Look at Year Nine. Dale has paid in $225,000 in premiums, and his cash value is $227,430. This is the point I call "break even." This is when he has more cash value than he has paid in premiums. Traditional whole life will take around 20 years to reach this point. It happens a lot faster when it's structured correctly for Infinite Banking.

3 Every loan repayment he makes increases what he can immediately borrow against. That is because the loan repayment goes toward principal. When you make the payment, the company releases that amount of cash value from collateral, and you then have access to immediately borrow against it again.

Dale is now 51 years old and can do whatever he wants with his cash value. He can continue buying rental properties, help pay for Jacob's wedding, pay for vacations, remodel the home or just sit on it and wait for a rainy day. Realistically, Dale would continue using this money, and, **regardless if he uses it or not, the projection remains the same at age 65**. So, for the sake of illustration, let's jump to age 66 when Dale decides to retire.

CASE STUDY - SUPPLEMENTING RETIREMENT

Dale is ready for retirement and knows exactly how much money he will have for it - no gambling here. He has $963,910 in this policy to supplement retirement as you can see on chart 14-2 on page 77. I say "this policy" because remember, any extra income had to go into a new policy and at some point a policy would have been started on Amy. There is not just one bank in town, they have branch locations, you will have the same through multiple policies.

Looking at the table on the next page you will see the outline of what Dale's retirement would look like. Dale figures he will live to be about 90 years old. That would allow him to borrow against $50,000 a year to supplement his retirement - income tax free, because it's borrowed money.

Don't forget, they also have the rental home from which they are getting monthly income. Remember from our tax buckets the income from the rental is passive income and is not taxed at the same rate as regular income.

Let's pause again and take a look at what is happening here in the policy during retirement.

1 Look at the Cash Value Difference column. You see, Dale is borrowing $50,000 from his policy each year, but his cash value is NOT decreasing by that same $50,000. This is because he is still earning compound interest, dividends and is still paying his premiums. Note the change in cash value column does not start decreasing by the amount he is borrowing until he is age 87.

2 Should he have received the same $50,000 from an IRA or 401k disbursement, he would have had to show this as ordinary income and pay tax on it. Most likely, he would have had to take out extra to pay the taxes, which would have depleted his investment in under 18 years. Using this allowed him to have access to money for 26 years and keep his tax burden down.

3 Even at age 92 he has $181,892 of death benefit to leave to his heirs. Had this money been in an investment, there

CHART 14-2

Age	Year	Premium	Distribution Amount	Net Cash Value	Change in Cash Value	Net Death Benefit
66	26	6,640	-50,000	911,890	11,187	1,764,840
67	27	6,640	-50,000	899.807	12,083	1,695,107
68	28	6,640	-50,000	886,824	12,983	1,626,870
69	29	6,640	-50,000	872,872	13,952	1,559,931
70	30	6,640	-50,000	857,915	14,957	1,494,192
71	31	6,640	-50,000	841,889	16,026	1,429,639
72	32	6,640	-50,000	824,714	17,175	1,366,315
73	33	6,640	-50,000	806,297	18,417	1,304,232
74	34	6,640	-50,000	786,625	19,672	1,243,243
75	35	6,640	-50,000	765,669	20,956	1,183,181
76	36	6,640	-50,000	743,408	22,261	1,123,927
77	37	6,640	-50,000	719,798	23,610	1,065,406
78	38	6,640	-50,000	694,768	25,030	1,007,592
79	39	6,640	-50,000	667,499	27,269	966,767
80	40	6,640	-50,000	637,827	29,672	923,819
81	41	6,640	-50,000	605,584	32,243	878,640
82	42	6,640	-50,000	570,584	35,000	831,073
83	43	6,640	-50,000	532,710	37,874	780.929
84	44	6,640	-50,000	491,790	40,920	728,045
85	45	6,640	-50,000	447,582	44,208	672,254
86	46	6,640	-50,000	399,783	47,799	613,354
87	47	6,640	-50,000	347,936	51,847	550,970
88	48	6,640	-50,000	291,615	56,321	484,700
89	49	6,640	-50,000	230,570	61,045	414,317
90	50	6,640	-50,000	164,569	66,001	339,623
91	51	6,640	-50,000	93,552	71,017	260,407
92	52	6,640	-44,815	22,925	70,627	181,892

would have been nothing left. On top of that, the death benefit goes to his heirs income-tax free.

Now you see how you can use your life insurance while you are alive for many things and still have money left for your heirs. How much is left depends on how much you use. All this is with tax advantages. It's about having access to cash today for what you need, access to cash tomorrow for retirement and taking care of your family when you are gone. What else can provide you those things while the money remains liquid and tax advantaged?

CASE STUDY - TEENS AND YOUNG ADULTS
(Loan interest applied in this case study)

Dale and Amy were already putting $1,000 a month away to help with Jacob's college tuition, so instead, they just redirected those same dollars into a life insurance policy on him, which you can see on the next page in graph 14-3. They started this when he was 13 years old. What they liked about this was that, not only was Jacob going to have access to this money for college, but he was going to be able to use this money for many things besides college if he was the kid that didn't want to go.

Dale and Amy owned this policy and Jacob was the insured, so they had all the control over the policy. Even though Dale and Amy owned it, the intent was to hand this ownership over to Jacob when he was older and mature enough to know what they intended for him. All kids mature at different levels, so that transfer date could be any time they saw fit.

Jacob used the cash value long before college. When he wanted his first car at 16 years old, Dale and Amy knew just where they were going to get that money - Jacob's policy. The cash value was $24,557, but they gave him a limit of $10,000 to spend. They knew this was the perfect time to teach Jacob how to be honest with his money by paying the policy back. They allowed

CHART 14-3

Age	Year	Premium	Cumulative Premium	Increase in Net Cash Value	Net Cash Value	Loan Amt Beg Year	Available Cash Value Beg Year	Loan Repayment	Available CV End Year	Death Benefit
14	1	12,000	12,000	7,874	7,874					832,225
15	2	12,000	24,000	8,187	16,061					903,955
16	3	12,000	36,000	8,497	-24,557	-10,000	14,557	1,200	15,757	973,601
17	4	12,000	48,000	10,128	34,686	-8,800	25,886	1,200	27,086	1,041,267
18	5	12,000	60,000	12,459	47,145	-7,600	39,545	2,400	41,945	1,107,060
19	6	12,000	72,000	12,903	60,048	-5,200	54,848	2,400	57,248	1,171,116
20	7	12,000	84,000	13,391	73,439	-2,800	70,639	2,800	73,439	1,233,565
21	8	12,000	96,000	13,917	87,356					1,294,468
22	9	12,000	108,000	14,474	101,830					1,353,852
23	10	12,000	120,000	15,071	116,901	-30,000	116,901	1,200	88,101	1,411,799
24	11	12,000	132,000	15,694	132,595	-28,800	103,795	1,200	104,995	1,468,381
25	12	12,000	144,000	16,354	148,949	-27,600	121,349	1,200	122,549	1,523,774
26	13	12,000	156,000	17,039	165,988	-26,400	139,588	1,200	140,788	1,578,024
27	14	12,000	168,000	17,742	183,730	-32,400	151,330	2,400	153,730	1,631,296
28	15	12,000	180,000	18,517	202,247	-30,000	172,247	2,400	174,647	1,683,629
29	16	12,000	192,000	19,349	221,596	-27,600	193,996	2,400	196,396	1,735,098
30	17	12,000	204,000	20,223	241,818	-65,200	176,615	2,400	179,018	1,785,586
31	18	12,000	216,000	21,129	262,947	-62,800	200,147	2,400	202,547	1,835,035
32	19	12,000	228,000	22,087	285,034	-60,400	224,634	2,100	246,734	1,883,467
33	20	12,000	240,000	23,070	308,104	-58,300	249,804	12,100	261,904	1,930,931
34	21	12,000	252,000	24,075	332,178	-46,200	285,978	7,680	293,658	1,977,462
35	22	12,000	264,000	25,137	357,315	-38,520	318,795	7,680	326,475	2,023,174
36	23	12,000	276,000	26,198	383,513	-30,840	352,673	7,680	360,353	2,068,140
37	24	12,000	288,000	27,269	410,782	-23,160	387,622	7,680	395,302	2,112,316
38	25	12,000	300,000	28,401	439,184	-15,480	423,704	7,680	431,384	2,155,781
39	26	12,000	312,000	29,498	468,682	-7,800	460,882	7,680	468,682	2,198,548
40	27	12,000	324,000	30,664	499,345					2,240,562
41	28	12,000	336,000	31,841	531,186	-80,000	451,186	0	451,186	2,281,851
42	29	12,000	348,000	33,037	564,223	-80,000	484,223	0	484,223	2,322,550
43	30	12,000	360,000	34,261	589,484	-80,000	518,494	5,000	523,484	2,362,704
44	31	12,000	372,000	35,496	633,981	-75,000	558,981	10,000	568,981	2,402,395
45	32	12,000	384,000	36,793	670,733	-65,000	605,733	20,000	625,733	2,441,797
46	33	12,000	396,000	38,126	708,899	-59,569	663,899	59,569	708,899	2,481,010
47	34	12,000	408,000	39,476	748,376					2,519,998
48	35	12,000	420,000	40,966	789,342					2,558,680
49	36	4,000	424,000	34,815	824,157					2,574,431
50	37	4,000	428,000	26,147	860,303					2,590,453
51	38	4,000	432,000	37,504	897,807					2,606,799
52	39	4,000	436,000	38,833	936,640					2,623,510
53	40	4,000	440,000	40,176	976,816					2,640,743
54	41	4,000	444,000	41,457	1,018,273					2,658,563
55	42	4,000	448,000	42,713	1,060,986					2,677,023
56	43	4,000	452,000	43,971	1,104,957					2,696,205
57	44	4,000	456,000	45,287	1,150,244					2,716,120
58	45	4,000	460,000	46,754	1,196,998					2,736,773
59	46	4,000	464,000	48,249	1,245,247					2,758,014
60	47	4,000	468,000	49,715	1,294,962					2,779,731
61	48	4,000	472,000	50,998	1,345,961					2,801,909
62	49	4,000	476,000	52,157	1,398,118					2,824,571
63	50	4,000	480,000	53,083	1,451,201					2,847,717
64	51	4,000	484,000	54,051	1,505,252					2,871,317
65	52	4,000	488,000	54,918	1,560,169					2,895,250

him to pay this back over five years, and they agreed he could afford $100 a month until he found a better paying job. Then he could make a balloon payment at the end. He could also pay more if he wanted. It was up to him, but it had to be paid off in five years.

Jacob paid the $1,200 a year until he was 18, at which time he increased his payment to $2,400 a year and then paid off the last year of $2,800.

Jacob didn't borrow against his cash value again until he was done with college. After he completed college at age 23, he decided to borrow $30,000 against his cash value to pay off his student loans. At this point his parents said they were done funding his policy. He was out of school, had a job and could fund it himself. Funding the policy and paying back student loans was a bit of a stretch, so he made the payments very minimal of $100 a month. He knew he could be flexible and pay more or less, since he did the same thing with the car repayment.

He paid this $1,200 a year for four years, is now 27 years old, and now wanted to buy an engagement ring for his girlfriend, Kylee. That was a loan for an additional $6,000, and he decided he could add another $100 a month to his payback. He was going to make this a 5 percent loan rate. So he had 69 months of payments. (Note: Year 19 of the illustration shows a $2,100 payment, $900 for the ring payoff and $1,200 for student loans.)

Jacob and Kylee got married a couple years later and decided to buy a house when he was 30 years old, so he borrowed against his cash value for the down payment from his policy, which was $40,000. They decided not to make any payments back for this loan at the time until they got the house all setup the way they wanted it. Moving into a new home always has some extra expenses, and they were warned not to over-extend themselves.

They began making payments back three years after they took the loan, when Jacob was 33 (Year 20 of the policy). Both he and Kylee had great jobs at this point and Kylee even got a sign-on bonus of $10,000 from her new job, which they applied as a loan repayment.

At age 33, Jacob still had $18,000 of student loans to repay and $30,000 for the house down payment. He wanted his student loans paid off in the next five years, so he increased his payment to $340 a month and decided they were going to put another $300 a month towards the down payment loan. So by age 39 they are doing well and only have $15,480 left to pay on what they borrowed for the down payment. Jacob's student loans are paid back in full!

However, they are used to making this $640 a month payment and they have two choices. They could either take that extra $340 a month and spend it elsewhere or just keep the loan repayment the same until their loan is paid off. There is only $7,800 left. This is when the teachings of being honest kicks in. Jacob decides to just keep paying the $640 a month. He knows he will have access to that money should he need it, and he also knows they are used to paying it, so why spend it foolishly? They would like to have a clean slate on the policy to start a new adventure. In fact, he decided to just pay the whole thing off and apply the extra $120 at the end of the year. IT'S TIME TO CELEBRATE!

They are debt free in Jacob's policy. What a great feeling, and Kylee has definitely learned a lot in the last several years about being honest with money. She had no idea it would work and was a bit leery when she met Jacob and he was telling her about this. Now she saw it in action and is ready to start her own policy.

Jacob is now 41 years old, has kids of his own and has been an employee now for many years. He has always dreamed of starting his own business, and he feels like now is the right time to do that. The kids are old enough that he can devote some time to taking on the new challenge. He needs $80,000 for startup equipment, rent, advertising and all the other expenses that come with starting a business. He also knows he won't be matching his current salary right away, so he will need some of that cash value for living expenses until he can get everything up and running.

Again, he does not make a payment back to himself for two years. His business has made enough to supplement his income for Year One but nothing extra to make payments. Year Three is getting better and he decided he could make a lump sum payment of $5,000 at the end of the year. Year Four was even better, and he was able to make a $10,000 payment. In Year Five, things took off like a rocket, and he was able to pay back $20,000. In Year Six, he tripled his income, and he paid back the remaining $59,569.

Note: he paid 5 percent interest on all his loans, and the interest did not increase his cash value, and that is if the life insurance company is charging the 5 percent to use their money. Should he have paid himself back at anything over 5 percent, he would have had extra cash value. This is what we mean when we talk about being an honest banker - paying yourself back more than what the life insurance company is charging you. Also note, when the illustration showed him not paying anything back at times, he should be paying interest only if he is unable to make a principal payment.

Jacob had $708,899 of cash value at this point, and we could go on and on about ways he could use that money. He can expand his business, buy properties, send the kids to college, pay for a wedding, and much more. At 65 years old, Jacob will have $1.5 million dollars. Again, just like his parents, his money will be used income-tax free.

Jacob was fortunate his parents started this for him when he was 13. Jacob also made some small sacrifices along the way, because he did have to pay his premium. However, he did not have to sacrifice as much as his peers who were contributing to a 401k. Jacob had access to his money immediately after he paid his premium, regardless if that was yearly or monthly. His peers were nowhere near able to put that kind of money away for retirement. They needed that money right away, and only saved what they had left over after all expenses were paid.

There's another law called Parkinson's Law. It is the fact that our needs will always rise to meet our income. R. Nelson Nash says, if you can beat Parkinson's Law, you will always be ahead of your peers. If you can get past that, you win.

Many of you may be saying you can't afford to start a policy on your kids at this age, much less put $12,000 a year into it. Okay, come back to **imagination, reason, and logic**. Do they have a part-time job where they can start funding their own policy? Do their grandparents give them money that you are putting into savings? It does not have to be $12,000 a year. It can be anything. Just get them started.

CASE STUDY - GRANDCHILD'S POLICY

Along the way Jacob and Kylee had a daughter named Emma. They could not afford another policy, but her Grandparents knew how important these policies are. So instead of giving their granddaughter money and unnecessary toys, they funded a policy for her.

They started right away when Emma was born. Not only did this allow for Emma to have accumulating cash value, but it also allowed for death benefit should anything happen to Emma. The death of a child is something I hope you never have to experience. Yet it happens, and most parents are not prepared for the financial loss that comes with a child.

As you can see on Chart 14-4, Dale and Amy were only putting in $1,200 a year for Emma, but she, too, will have money for a car, college, and other needs. Emma will also learn how to be honest with her money by borrowing against her policy and paying it back. She will have to go to her grandparents to do so, but who better to teach her how to handle money than those who have already done it?

CHART 14-4

Age	Year	Premium	Cumulative Premium	Increase in Net Cash Value	Net Cash Value	Death Benefit
1	1	1,200	1,200	687	687	152,356
5	5	1,200	6,000	824	3,767	203,436
10	10	1,200	12,000	1,447	10,094	257,579
15	15	1,200	18,000	1,726	18,209	302,708
20	20	1,200	24,000	1,994	27,546	341,152
25	25	1,200	30,000	2,454	38,859	374,271
30	30	1,200	36,000	3,037	52,781	402,869
40	40	500	46,600	3,907	90,214	442,359
50	50	500	51,600	5,470	137,333	451,805

CASE STUDY - USING INHERITANCE OR LARGE SUMS OF CASH

You never know if you will have a windfall of money and a lot of times it comes very unexpectedly. It could come with something like winning the lottery, and you will want to be very wise with this money.

Amy's mother passed away when Amy was 55 years old and left her with $500,000 of inheritance. This money came to Amy through a death benefit her mother had. Since she and Dale had used this concept for a number of years already, they knew it was the best place to put their money. They were not sure they could fund another policy for the rest of their lives, so this one was set up to move the $500,000 into a policy over a seven-year period.

CHART 14-5

Age	Year	Premium	Cumulative Premium	Increase in Net Cash Value	Net Cash Value	Death Benefit
56	1	110,000	110,000	88,340	88,340	2,016,644
57	2	110,000	220,000	92,909	181,248	2,246,906
58	3	65,000	285,000	67,254	248,502	2,363,389
59	4	65,000	350,000	69,830	318,333	2,478,451
60	5	65,000	415,000	72,503	390,836	2,592,270
61	6	65,000	480,000	75,257	466,093	2,704,932
62	7	20,000	500,000	34,073	500,166	2,718,751
63	8	0	500,000	20,318	520,484	1,124,207
64	9	0	500,000	21,030	541,513	1,137,519
65	10	0	500,000	21,723	563,236	1,151,056
66	11	0	500,000	22,418	585,654	1,164,790
67	12	0	500,000	23,104	608,759	1,178,714
68	13	0	500,000	23,792	632,550	1,192,813
69	14	0	500,000	24,468	657,019	1,207,073
70	15	0	500,000	25,121	682,139	1,221,479
71	16	0	500,000	25,747	707,887	1,236,008
72	17	0	500,000	26,347	734,233	1,250,674
73	18	0	500,000	26,919	761,152	1,265,470
74	19	0	500,000	27,474	788,626	1,280,355
75	20	0	500,000	27,997	816,623	1,295,326
76	21	0	500,000	28,462	845,085	1,310,341
77	22	0	500,000	28,918	874,003	1,325,384
78	23	0	500,000	29,337	903,340	1,340,441
79	24	0	500,000	29,745	933,085	1,355,501
80	25	0	500,000	30,100	963,185	1,370,527

Chart 14-5 on the previous page shows that by the end of Year Seven, Amy has access to the full $500,000 she has put in as premiums. What is even more exciting is even without continued premiums the cash value continues to grow by at least $20,000 each year! By the time she is 70 years old, Amy has $182,000 more in cash value than what she put into the policy. She has $682,000 to borrow against to supplement retirement.

This is an easy one to break down. If Amy should pass away at 80 years old, she will leave $1.3 million of death benefit to her heirs. This $1.3 million was purchased with $500,000 of money she received income tax free from her mother's death benefit. She is now leaving it to her heirs in the form of $1.3 million income tax free. That means every dollar of death benefit was purchased for only $0.36! Where else are you going to go to buy discounted dollars, income-tax free?

Setting up a policy in this manner is not only for inheritance of death benefit, it is also used for those sitting on large amounts of accessible money. **The more money put in up front, the faster the policy breaks even and the faster the compounding happens.**

This policy was illustrated to only pay premium for seven years. However, Amy could have continued paying a $15,000 premium to keep the policy active, which is yet another benefit of using the properly structured dividend paying whole life policy with an agent that is certified in IBC and understands this. Not all companies offer this flexibility, and it's very important to work with a certified IBC agent.

FAMILY BANKING

When policies are started on all the family members, it is called a family banking system. Parents can't always afford to start policies on their kids, but they can normally start them on their grandkids. It may have to skip a generation, where grandparents start one on themselves and their grandkids, and the kids start one on themselves. Either way, everyone is covered, and the family banking system has begun. You can lend money within the family with strict banking rules that it must be paid back and with interest. In the end, it all goes to the families' estate. Win. Win. The knowledge will be transferred to the next generation to insure generational wealth.

I use the story of the Vanderbilt and the Rothschild families as an example. In 1877, Cornelius Vanderbilt died the richest man in the United States, leaving an estate of $105 million to his heirs. By 1973 there was not one Vanderbilt left that was a millionaire.

Yet, the Rothschild family has experienced something different. When Amschel Rothschild died in 1812, he had set up a banking dynasty for his heirs. Prior to passing, he taught his five sons conservative money management. They borrowed from a family banking system and were taught to pay it back each time they borrowed. The key word is taught. Mr. Rothschild passed on his financial knowledge. Today the Rothschild dynasty is valued in the trillions.

Research shows that family money rarely survives the transfer for long, with 70 percent evaporated by the end of the second generation. By the end of the third generation, 90 percent will have evaporated. Think about what you can teach your family for future success. Leaving a legacy of knowledge is priceless.

> ***Get more information by listening to Mary Jo's podcast, Without the Bank.***

CHAPTER FIFTEEN

Your Next Step

"Action is the foundational key to all success."
- Pablo Picasso

What is your next step? It's action. Call to make an appointment with me or check your emails for a link to my calendar so you can get started correctly with someone who understands the concept, how to set the policy up, and will be there to help you with strategies during your lifetime.

Everyone has potential to apply this concept. The truth is that not everyone will for the simple reason they are wishful instead of willful in their thinking or paralyzed with fear. While the wishful enjoy the idea of wealth, the willful take the actions that lead to wealth. Again, like my client Nate said, **"it's easy when you stop making it so hard."**

Be careful who you use to implement this concept. I would venture to say 99.9 percent of agents have not heard of this nor understand it. Yet, they will look at the numbers and tell you they can do this. Surely they don't want to give up a commission!

I understand you most likely already have an agent or a relationship with one you want to support. That is noble, but if you truly care about your finances you'll find an agent who is certified to teach this concept. Remember, the policy is the tool to the concept. If your agent can't continue to teach you how to think differently and use the policy, what good is the policy? It's like having a hammer without the nails. Good luck building that home.

It's amazing how many policies I look at that were setup by local agents, friends who are agents or existing family agents - and they are WRONG! They are either the wrong life insurance product or just flat out wrong. Yet these agents said they could do it. I then get the SOS call on what to do. It may be too late, and money is lost.

I'd love to see you experience financial success, so please take your money seriously, think like a bank owner, and set an appointment up with me so you can learn how to implement the concept for a life without the bank.

DO YOUR DUE DILIGENCE

If you do not visit with me, be sure to ask the following questions of the agent you decide to work with:

Q. Do you understand whole life versus permanent life?
Q. Do you recommend whole life?
Q. Do you have a whole life policy yourself?
Q. Do you know what a Paid Up Additions rider is and how it works?
Q. Do you know what Modified Endowment Contract means?
Q. Do you work with mutual companies who pay dividends?
Q. What is the financial rating of your company?
Q. What does the insurance company's portfolio look like?

If agents are answering these questions and you hear any of the following comments or words, you'd better either run away quickly or think long and hard about what you want to do:

- "Yes, in our "whole life" you can make an 8-12 percent rate of return." Remember, some agents call Universal, Variable and the mixes of the two, whole life. They have the terminology wrong - those are permanent life products, NOT whole life. Getting that wrong is a huge red flag.
- Surrender charge

- No guarantees
- Death benefit does not increase over the years
- Illustrations that don't show at least 60 percent of your premium available in cash value year one.
- Premium is only paid 10 or 20 years.
- Policy is a paid up at 65, no more premiums due after age 65.
- They do not work with mutual dividend paying companies.
- Their company rating is lower than an A-.
- "Whole life agents line their pockets with commission."
- "Whole life is expensive. Term is the cheaper, invest the difference."

FREQUENTLY ASKED QUESTIONS

If you are like most people who hear of this, you may have the following common questions.

Q. How much money do I need to start?
A. You can start with just about any amount. Your financial situation determines what is right for you. You just want to be sure the premium is affordable and you can continue to pay it each year.

Q. Where do I find this money to start with?
A. Do you have money going to or in a savings account, investment, or retirement accounts? Are you overpaying on debt or just finished paying something off?

Q. Is there a limit to how much I can pay?
A. Yes. In a properly structured whole life policy, the amount you can put in is determined by your human life value. This is a factor of your gross income times 30, 20, 15 or 10, depending on

your age. If you can't get enough on yourself, you may be able to insure others with whom you have an insurable interest.

Q. How much do I have to pay every year?
A. This amount is flexible and there is a minimum premium that must be paid. I wish it was an easy number, but it changes with every person. When you start a policy you will know this amount down to the penny.

Q. What happens if I don't pay the full premium?
A. It's okay as long as you pay the minimum premium.

Q. What happens if there is a loan on the policy and I die?
A. If you are the insured and there is a loan, your heirs will get the death benefit minus the cash value loan and interest.

Q. Do my heirs get the cash value and the death benefit upon my death?
A. No, they do not. The cash value is the net present value of the death benefit.

Q. Why haven't I heard of this before?
A. That is a really good question, one that I also had when I first heard of this concept. I do not have a perfect answer for you, but I can tell you a few things I think contribute to this. The first would be because of the births of the 401k and IRA in the 1970s and 1980s that I talk about earlier in the book. This has led to our conditioned thinking that investing is the traditional retirement plan. Secondly, I believe it attributed to the misconception to buy term and invest the difference, which caused people to cancel their whole life during this time and replace it with market driven products. And third, life insurance companies have done a poor

job of training agents that have agencies. As a result, very few people under the age of 45 have ever been exposed to cash value life insurance and, on top of that, the number of life insurance agents we have across the country are decreasing.

Q. Are all whole life policies and companies the same?
A. No, no and no! Properly structured policies are specifically designed to accelerate cash value growth. They have riders added that allows for this and not all companies have these riders or offer the flexibility needed to maximize them. Also, the company must be mutual with a good rating and financial history.

Q. I already have a whole life policy. Can I use that?
A. Yes, if it has cash value. If it's a true whole life policy and you have had it for years, you will most likely have some cash value there. It's always a bonus when new clients have existing cash value.

Q. What is the risk involved? It sounds too good to be true.
A. It would be wrong to say there is no risk. There are three factors that can affect this. One, the life insurance company could go under. This should not be a concern if you are working with a stable company, for example, the companies I work with are more than 140 years old, conservative and have well-managed portfolios. Two, there is human nature. This is the riskiest part of it all. If you are pre-retirement age and take a loan and don't repay it or interest, your policy may lapse. Three, would be buying the wrong life insurance policy from agents who have no idea what they are doing.

Q. Are you just a life insurance agent just trying to sell insurance?
A. No. I am a life insurance agent certified in teaching the Infinite Banking Concept® that happens to use the tool of properly struc-

tured whole life insurance from a mutual company. The intent for the book is to educate you and open your eyes to the financial noise you are being conditioned with. Once clients buy a policy they become lifelong students of mine. I continue to service them and teach them new strategies and thought processes needed to create a life without the bank. A life insurance agent will sell you a policy and walk away. You NEED a lifelong teacher of this concept.

NOTES

The concept is easy, but it is not easy to grasp it all on the first read. Please read and re-read this book several times. Each time you read it you will hear something new and you'll find a few "ah ha" moments.

You've heard me talk about R. Nelson Nash throughout this book. If you truly want to understand this concept, add his book Becoming Your Own Banker to your reading list. That book in conjunction with this book would be a great start to a full education of what this is, why it works and how to use it.

I'd like to thank you for reading, and since you made it to the end I trust you found this book to be worthy of your time. Please feel free to contact me and schedule your FREE consultation to see how this can work in your life.

Contact me at *maryjo@withoutthebank*, visit the website at *www.withoutthebank.com* or give me a call at 701-751-3917. You also get emails from me with links to my calendar and can schedule there.

All calculators used were from Truth Concepts.
www.truthconcepts.com

ABOUT THE AUTHOR

Mary Jo is a lifelong entrepreneur who worked for someone else and never bought into the traditional financial planning. After many years of looking for answers for a better way to utilize her money she found the Infinite Banking Concept and has been teaching that since 2010. As and employee she realized she was not going to be able to retire off the stock market and company matches that the traditional planners touted for being the answer. Now as an entrepreneur she understands the frustration and B.S. one has to go through when trying to get a loan from banks. Because she's been on both sides she knows employees are being lied to and entrepreneur's are being held back due to traditional finance. She is now on a mission to teach the truth!

She was in your shoes, she was looking for those answers, found them and then questioned everything she just read. How could any of this be true, if it was why hadn't she heard about it? Please know, any question you have reading this book, Mary Jo had it too. Weeks were spent reading every book she could get her hand on and now years have been spent learning and teaching this concept to others. It is true, it can be done and you just need to be open to hearing it.

Mary Jo is also a bestselling author of the book Farming Without the Bank, which has sold over 12,000 copies as a self published book, a speaker and financial strategist.

She hopes to meet you someday and hear your story. She LOVES visiting with clients, near and far, and learning about what they do. Virtual meeting has brought her into living rooms and kitchens all around the world!

RECOMMENDED READINGS

Becoming Your Own Banker by R. Nelson Nash
Building Your Warehouse of Wealth by R. Nelson Nash
Financial Peace of Mind by Dwayne Burnell
Great Wall Street Retirement Scam by Rick Bueter
Financial Independence in the 21st Century
by Dwayne and Suzanne Burnell
How Privatized Banking Really Works
by L. Carlos Lara and Robert P. Murphy

DISCLAIMER

The illustrations in this book are for educational purposes only. Illustrations do not represent any particular insurance company or have any kind of guarantees associated with them. They are intended for teaching purposes only.

Exact numbers are not guaranteed, as results will change based on age, gender, health, state, company and type of insurance, as well as other conditions. This book does not represent any insurance company in particular.

Illustrations in this book assume payment of dividends for all years shown. However, dividends are not guaranteed and may be declared annually by the insurance company's board of directors. Dividends fluctuate, and, there-fore, can be higher or lower than illustrated. All illustrations were run as NO MECs (modified endowment con-tracts) allowing all loans against the cash value to be income tax free.

The Infinite Banking Concept® is a registered trademark of Infinite Banking Concepts, LLC. FiscalBridge, LLC, is independent of and is not affiliated with, sponsored by, or en-dorsed by Infinite Banking Concepts, LLC.